COOKING WITH KALE

Cooking with
KALE

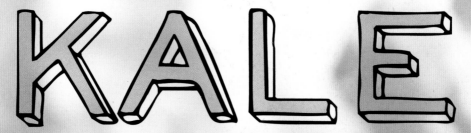

Rena Patten

NEW
HOLLAND

Dedication

For Madison, Kobe, Isaac, Hudson and Cooper.

Published in 2015 by
New Holland Publishers
London • Sydney • Auckland

The Chandlery Unit 114 50 Westminster Bridge Road London SE1 7QY United Kingdom
1/66 Gibbes Street Chatswood NSW 2067 Australia
5 39 Woodside Ave Northcote Auckland New Zealand

www.newhollandpublishers.com

A catalogue record of this book is available at the British Library and the National Library of Australia.

ISBN: 9781742576718

Managing Director: Fiona Schultz
Publisher: Linda Williams
Project Editor: Simona Hill
Cover Design: Lorena Susak
Design: Andrew Davies
Production Director: Olga Dementiev
Printer: Toppan Leefung Printing Ltd (China)

10 9 8 7 6 5 4 3 2 1

Follow New Holland Publishers on
Facebook: www.facebook.com/NewHollandPublishers

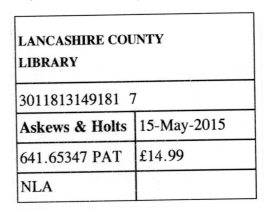

Acknowledgments

I would like to say a huge thank you to my friend and publisher Linda Williams, and to Fiona Schultz, Managing Director of New Holland, for giving me the opportunity to write this book. I am very grateful for, and appreciate your continued support, trust, encouragement and belief in my work. Thank you, too, to Olga Dementiev, Lucia Donnelly, Diane Ward, Simona Hill, Victor Yoog, Susie Stevens, Lorena Susak and Andrew Davies from New Holland. It is always such a pleasure to work with New Holland; you make the process of publishing a book painless. I cannot thank you all enough for your help and hard work.

A very special thank you to food stylist Tracy Rutherford and photographer Sue Stubbs; it is such a pleasure working with both of you. You make the long, hard days of the photoshoot such a breeze and you always manage to bring my food to life by making it look exactly as it should.

Special thanks to Linda Jones, her wonderful family, and to all the staff at Alfresco Emporium at Collaroy, Sydney, Australia. Your never-ending support for all my books and my cooking demonstrations is so very much appreciated. It is such a joy to hold cooking demonstrations in your special store among beautiful home and kitchenware. Beautiful kitchenware from Alfresco Emporium features in the some of the photographs in this book.

To my wonderful and very special family – my husband Graeme, my children Alex, Nikki, and Christopher, their other halves Lachlan, Marcus and Carolyn, and to my gorgeous grandchildren Madison, Kobe, Isaac, Hudson and Cooper, and to my parents, thank you for your love, patience, understanding and support in all that I do.

CONTENTS

Introduction

Whenever I am out buying kale, I am amazed at how many people stop and ask me how I intend to prepare this green leafy vegetable. Invariably they always state that they know kale is good for them and that they want to try it but have no idea what to do with it. So many people appeared to think that the best and only uses for kale were to either boil or steam it and serve it as an accompaniment to a dish, or blend it into a smoothie. Kale prepared correctly is a beautiful tasting vegetable, and a firm favourite in my family. This book will show you the many different ways that kale can be prepared and enjoyed by all the family; my young grandchildren absolutely love it. I hope that the recipes included in this book will help you dispel any misconceptions that you may have about this delicious vegetable, and banish any unpleasant memory or association that you have. When cooked correctly, I hope that you will be very pleasantly surprised by its taste. You'll also have the added bonus of knowing that it is good for you.

Kale is a member of the cabbage family (Brassicaceae), a group of cruciferous leafy vegetables and one of the world's dominant food groups. Brassicas include kale, cabbage, cauliflower, kohl rabi, bok choy, Brussels sprouts and some seeds such as mustard, to name a few. All vegetables from this family have significant health benefits when eaten regularly, and kale, in particular, is a nutritional powerhouse.

The Health Benefits

This frilly leafed, highly nutritious green vegetable has surged in popularity of late as the health benefits associated with it have become more widely publicised. Kale is often referred to as a 'superfood', a term that helps define foods that are densely packed with nutrients, such as highly powerful antioxidants, vitamins, minerals and essential fatty acids that, when incorporated into the diet, will help to nourish the body, promoting health from the inside out. Although all vegetables contain vital nutrients and are good for us, some, such as kale, contain greater nutritional value, so it makes sense to incorporate these more regularly into our diets.

The main health benefits of kale are linked to the high concentration of antioxidants, phytonutrients and vitamins A, C, and K that it contains. Kale is high in natural antioxidants, meaning that eating it can help may help reduce, neutralize and even prevent free radical cells in our bodies that can cause harm. Beta-carotene, one of the main antioxidants found in kale, is thought, by many nutritional experts, to help contribute in the fight against cancer by blocking and destroying cancer cell growth. Kale also contains high concentrations of carotenoids and flavonoids, which are antioxidants that can help our bodies expel free radicals and also help protect us in the fight against cancer.

Kale is rich in omega 3 fatty acids, which are essential in reducing inflammation and swelling in the body. Omega 3 is known to boost brain function.

The sulphur in the kale and high fibre helps detoxify the body and keep the liver healthy. Kale is a rich source of minerals such as calcium, copper, iron, potassium, folate, manganese and phosphorous. Being rich in vitamin K, it helps promotes bone formation and strengthening, and normal healthy blood clotting. Kale is also very high in calcium, which is helpful in preventing bone loss. It can help limit damage to brain cells and can aid in the prevention of calcium build-up in the arteries. Kale is thought to help reduce blood cholesterol levels and may reduce the risk of heart disease due to its high fibre content that binds bile acids together.

If eaten regularly as part of a balanced diet, kale may help to ward off disease. It is thought that the unusually high amounts of nutrients it contains may help to reduce the risk of heart disease, cancer, high blood pressure, high cholesterol and obesity. Eating it regularly will instil a feeling of physical and emotional wellbeing.

It is thought that kale has a higher iron content than beef. Iron is needed to produce haemoglobin, which is essential for transporting oxygen through the bloodstream, for proper liver function and for general good health.

Precaution: It should be noted that kale contains certain components that may interfere with blood thinning medications. If you are taking such medication, it is advisable to monitor your intake of kale and consult your doctor for advice.

Kale is fat free, so can help with weight control. Like other vegetables, it is also low in calories.

Varieties of Kale

The most common type of kale, and the one most readily available, is curly kale. The second most common variety is lacinato kale, also known as Italian cavolo nero, Tuscan kale or dinosaur kale. Baby kale is also now available at most major supermarkets, which is ideal for eating raw in salads. Just wash and dry the leaves. Standard kale can also be eaten a salad leaves and combines particularly well with other salad ingredients.

Cultivated ornamental kale is also available with white, purple or green leaves.

When buying kale look for bunches that have firm and thick deep green leaves. Choose stalks that have small leaves as they are more tender and milder in taste. Avoid bunches that have leaves with holes in them, yellow leaves or those that look soft and as if they are wilting. Kale will keep for a few days in the refrigerator, I usually loosely wrap it in a plastic bag before storing it in the refrigerator and I never wash it until just before I am about to use it. For the purposes of the recipes in this book, a large bunch usually has 8-10 large stalks.

Preparation

Kale has its own distinct flavour and its intensity can vary from one variety to another. It has a pleasant, mild, sometimes very slight bitter flavour and an odour and taste that have a hint of cabbage with maybe a bit of broccoli. Curly kale has strong, thick, tight leaves, and although it collapses when cooked, it does not tend to lose its texture or shape. Tuscan kale can have a slightly stronger taste, that is more similar to cabbage than the curly variety, and a taste that reminds me of the leaves that you sometimes find on broccoli. It has stronger, thicker, flatter, knobbly leaves.

Baby kale, on the other hand, is totally different. It is a small, delicate and fresh leaf with a very subtle and light taste that can be slightly peppery and reminds me of rocket (arugula). On the whole, the overall taste of kale changes from dish to dish depending on how it is prepared and what it is prepared with.

The best way to prepare kale is to thoroughly wash it, remove the thick,

tough stalks, then chop the leaves as finely as possible, or tear the leaves into small pieces. The quickest way to remove the stalk is to hold the end of it in one hand, and with the other hand, grab the leaf at the same end, and in one movement quickly pull the leaf along the stem from the lower part of the stem to the top. You will find that the tough part of the stalk easily separates leaving the upper more tender part of the stalk attached to the leaves. Alternatively cut out most of the stalk with a knife. The upper, more tender part of the stalk is perfectly good to use and I usually do so in all my recipes. I prefer to use a large wide-surfaced frying pan or when cooking kale until it wilts.

As with most leafy greens, kale starts to shrink in volume once it comes into contact with heat or liquid, so prepare more than you think you will need.

Tip: I always use a large chopping board when working with kale because it tends to spread out.

Uses of Kale

Kale is very versatile. It adds colour, flavour and liquid to juices and smoothies. It can be used in soups, salads, casseroles, pies, muffins, omelettes, stir-fries and stuffing and is even great when incorporated into homemade pasta dough. It is a wonderful vegetable for vegetarians and beneficial for those following a vegan lifestyle. For snacks, it can be made into 'chips' or 'crisps' as an alternative to higher calorie potato chips.

Some people are reluctant to use kale in salads because the taste is a little too sharp. To rectify this, after washing and chopping the kale, mix the dressing ingredients to be used in the salad, then rub some of the dressing into the leaves. Set aside the kale for a while before adding the remaining salad ingredients and dressing to the salad. Rubbing the dressing into the kale with your hands softens the kale and makes it more palatable. Alternatively, you could blanche the kale leaves in boiling water for 2-3 minutes before refreshing the leaves under cold running water. Dry thoroughly before chopping the leaves and adding to the salad.

Why not give kale a try? I think you will be pleasantly surprised at the number of dishes you can create with it.

The Recipes

BREAKFAST and SMOOTHIES

Banana, Chia and Kale Smoothie

Mixed Berry and Kale Smoothie

Buttermilk, Bacon and Kale Pancakes

Sweet Potato and Kale Pancakes

Kale with Chorizo Sausage and Eggs

Mushroom, Tomato, Avocado and Poached Egg on Toast

Potato, Bacon and Corn Kale Fritters

Roasted Capsicum, Feta and Kale Muffins

Ginger, Carrot and Orange Smoothie

Ham, Zucchini and Cheese Muffins

Scrambled Eggs with Kale, Chorizo Sausage and Cottage Cheese

Banana, Chia and Kale Smoothie

Prepare this smoothie just before serving and drink straightaway before it starts to lose its vibrant green colour. Adjust the amount of chia seeds and level of sweetness used to suit your taste.

2 large stalks of kale
1 banana, peeled and sliced
2 stalks celery, roughly
    chopped
1½ cups (12 fl oz/375 ml)
    apple juice
1-2 tablespoons chia seeds
2 teaspoons honey or
    agave syrup
1 small Lebanese cucumber,
    sliced
6-8 mint leaves
1 tablespoon lemon juice
1-2 cups (5-10 oz/150-
    280 g) ice cubes

Thoroughly wash the kale, remove and discard the tough lower part of the stalks and roughly chop the leaves. Place the kale into a blender with all the other ingredients and blend until smooth, thick and creamy.

Serve immediately.

Mixed Berry and Kale Smoothie

The intensity of the colour of this smoothie will depend on the type of mixed berries used. For this recipe, I used a mixture of strawberries, raspberries, blueberries and blackberries.

Thoroughly wash the kale and remove the thick tough lower part of the stalk. Roughly chop the leaves and put in a blender with all the other ingredients.

Blend until smooth, thick and creamy.

Taste, and adjust the level of sweetness, by adding a little more honey, if you like. Serve immediately.

3 stalks of kale

2 cups (16 fl oz/500 ml) coconut water

1-2 teaspoons organic raw coconut oil

2 tablespoons honey or agave syrup, plus a little extra, if needed

2 cups (9 oz/250 g) frozen mixed berries

Few sprigs of mint

Note: Fresh mangoes can be substituted for the berries.

Buttermilk, Bacon and Kale Pancakes

For a vegetarian option leave out the bacon and add either grated Cheddar (tasty) cheese or crumbled feta or goats' cheese. If you are a meat eater you could substitute chorizo sausage for the bacon.

Thoroughly wash the kale, remove and discard the entire stalk. Finely chop the leaves and set aside.

Heat the oil in a large frying pan, add the bacon and onions and cook until soft.

Add the kale, season with salt and pepper and continue cooking 3–5 minutes, stirring occasionally, until the kale wilts and is cooked. Stir in the garlic and cook for a few seconds. Set aside to cool slightly.

In a small bowl, whisk together the buttermilk, eggs and mustard.

Sift the flour and baking powder into another large bowl and make a well in the center. Slowly pour in the buttermilk mixture, whisking at the same time, until you have a smooth batter without any lumps. Stir in the kale and bacon.

Heat a medium-large non-stick frying pan until hot over medium heat. Brush with a little melted butter and pour in about one-third of a cup (2½ fl oz/75 ml) of the batter into the pan.

Cook the pancakes in batches until bubbles start to appear and the top is almost set. Flip over and cook until the other side is set.

Remove and place onto a plate, cover with foil and keep warm until all the pancakes are cooked. Wipe the pan clean with kitchen paper between each batch of pancakes. Serve warm with maple syrup.

6 stalks of kale

1–2 tablespoons extra virgin olive oil

3 rashers (strips) bacon, rind removed and finely chopped

4 shallots/spring onions/ scallions, finely sliced

Salt and freshly cracked black pepper

1–2 garlic cloves, finely chopped (optional)

1 pint (600 ml) buttermilk

2 extra large eggs

2 teaspoons English mustard or horseradish

2 cups (1 lb/450 g) self-rising (self-raising) flour

1 teaspoon baking powder

Melted butter, for cooking

Maple syrup, for serving

Sweet Potato and Kale Pancakes

MAKES ABOUT 12

Note: I like to cook the sweet potato by baking it whole with the skin on in the oven until soft when tested with a skewer. Peel when cool enough to handle then mash with a fork. You can also boil or steam the potato if you prefer.

6-8 stalks of kale
2 tablespoons extra virgin olive oil
1 small red onion, finely chopped
1 garlic clove, finely grated
1 cup (4 oz/115 g) self-rising (self-raising) flour
½ teaspoon ground cumin
1 teaspoon baking powder
17 oz (500 g) sweet potato (kumera), cooked and mashed
2 extra-large eggs
Salt and freshly cracked black pepper
1½ cups (12 fl oz/375 ml) milk
Butter or extra virgin olive oil, for cooking

DRESSING

1 cup (8 fl oz/250 ml) Greek (strained plain) yogurt
1-2 tablespoons fresh mint, chopped
1 teaspoon extra virgin olive oil

Thoroughly wash the kale, remove and discard the thick lower part of the stalk and finely chop the leaves.

Heat the oil in a large frying pan and sauté the onion until soft. Stir in the garlic and kale and cook for 3-5 minutes, until the kale is tender. Remove from the heat, place into a bowl and cool slightly.

Sift the flour, cumin and baking powder together into a bowl and add to the kale with the potato, eggs, salt and pepper.

Slowly pour in the milk and mix well until all the ingredients are thoroughly combined and you have a thick batter.

Heat a non-stick frying pan on medium heat until hot and brush with butter or oil.

Pour about 2½ fl oz (75 ml) of the batter at a time into the pan and fry the pancake until bubbles start to appear and the top is set, about 2-3 minutes.

Flip over the pancake and fry until the other side is set. Keep the pancakes warm while you repeat the process and all of the batter is used.

For the dressing, mix together the yogurt, mint and olive oil, and season with salt and pepper. Serve the pancakes with a dollop of the mint yogurt.

Kale with Chorizo Sausage and Eggs

This dish is ideal for breakfast, brunch, lunch or a light supper.

Thoroughly wash the kale, remove and discard the thick lower part of the stalk and finely chop the leaves. Set aside.

Heat the oil in a large frying pan and cook the chorizo until golden all over, remove from the pan and set aside. Discard any excess oil keeping only about a tablespoon or so.

Add the onions, garlic and chilli, if using, to the pan and sauté for 1–2 minutes, until golden.

Add the tomatoes and their juice and kale, season with salt and pepper and cook for 3–4 minutes until the kale starts to wilt.

Add the water, cover and cook for about 5–8 minutes, until the kale is tender.

Return the chorizo sausage to the pan and combine with the kale.

Make 4 wells in the mixture in the pan and gently crack an egg into each one.

Cook on gentle heat until the eggs are set to your liking. Check and adjust the seasoning and serve with crusty bread.

4–6 stalks of kale
1 tablespoon extra virgin olive oil
1–2 chorizo sausages (about 9 oz/250 g total weight), sliced
4 shallots/spring onions/ scallions finely chopped
1 garlic clove, chopped
½ teaspoon dried chilli flakes (optional)
1 x 14 oz (400 g) can diced tomatoes
Salt and freshly cracked black pepper
½ cup (4 fl oz/125 ml) water
4 eggs
Crusty bread, to serve

Note: If you are gluten or wheat intolerant check the ingredients in the chorizo sausage for wheat products.

Mushroom, Tomato, Avocado and Poached Egg on Toast

SERVES 2

This is an ideal dish for brunch.

6 stalks of kale
1-2 tablespoons extra virgin
   olive oil
1-2 teaspoons butter
9 oz (250 g) mushrooms,
   thickly sliced
4 oz (125 g) grape or
   cherry tomatoes
14 shallots/spring onions/
   scallions, sliced
1 garlic clove, grated
Salt and freshly cracked
   black pepper
2 eggs
2 large slices of bread
1 avocado, sliced
Balsamic vinegar

Thoroughly wash the kale, remove the thick lower part of the stalk and tear the leaves into pieces. Set aside.

Heat the oil and melt the butter together in a large frying pan and sauté the mushrooms until tender.

Add the tomatoes, onions and garlic and continue cooking until the tomatoes start to blister.

Stir in the kale, season with salt and pepper and cook for 3-5 minutes until the kale softens and it is cooked. If necessary, add about 1-2 tablespoonful of water to create some steam for the kale to cook quicker.

In the meantime, poach the eggs and toast the bread.

When the kale and toast are ready, place half the kale and mushrooms on each slice of toast, top with slices of avocado and a poached egg.

Season the egg and avocado with a little salt, a good grind of pepper and a drizzle of extra virgin olive oil and balsamic vinegar.

Note: Slices of prosciutto lightly crisped in a pan or under a grill (broiler) goes really well in this dish.

Potato, Bacon, and Corn Kale Fritters

Delicious for brunch, these fritters are quick to make and very easy to eat!

Thoroughly wash the kale and remove the thick lower part of the stalk, finely chop the leaves. Set aside

Preheat the oven to 200°C/400°F/Gas mark 6 and line 2 baking sheets with non-stick baking or parchment paper.

Peel and coarsely grate the potatoes then squeeze out as much of their starchy moisture as possible. This is sometimes best done by wrapping the grated potato in a clean kitchen towel and squeezing. The potatoes should be as dry as possible. Place the potatoes into a bowl with the kale.

Finely slice the onions and finely chop the bacon. Add both to the potatoes and kale along with the corn kernels and garlic.

Mix in the eggs, mustard and flour and season with salt and pepper.

Place about 2 tablespoons of the potato and kale mixture in heaps to form a fritter on the prepared baking sheet and bake for 15–20 minutes, until golden and cooked.

Serve warm with a dollop of sour cream and a sprinkle of chopped chives.

6 stalks of kale
4 large potatoes, about 1 lb 10 oz (750 g)
4 shallots/spring onions/ scallions
2 rashers (strips) bacon
1 cup (6 oz/175 g) sweet corn kernels
1 garlic clove, finely chopped
4 extra large eggs, lightly beaten
1 tablespoon English mustard
3 tablespoons flour
Salt and freshly cracked black pepper
Sour cream, for serving
Chopped chives, for garnish

Note: For a vegetarian option leave out the bacon. If you prefer not to bake the fritters they can be cooked in a non-stick frying pan with a little olive oil. I find that when they are cooked this way they tend to brown fairly quickly but the potato is still not quite cooked.

Roasted Capsicum, Feta and Kale Muffins

MAKES 12 REGULAR MUFFINS

As you can see in the photograph, for fun I baked these muffins in small terra cotta pots specially designed for cooking – these pots have no drainage hole in the base, unlike gardening pots. The pots stand 2½ in (6.5 cm) tall x 2¾ in (7 cm) wide. I cut rectangles of non-stick baking paper to line them. Lightly grease the pots so that the paper sticks to them, then push the paper, from the middle, into the pots. Pleat to fit. Fill the pots to just above the rim.

4 stalks cavolo nero (Tuscan kale)
5 oz (150 g) fire-roasted capsicums (bell peppers), finely chopped
3 oz (90 g) feta cheese
2 shallots/spring onions/scallions, sliced
1 garlic clove, grated
1-2 tablespoons grated Parmesan
2 cups (1 lb/450 g) self-rising (self-raising) flour
2 extra-large eggs, lightly beaten
1 cup (8 fl oz/250 ml) low-fat (semi-skimmed) milk
4½ oz (125 g) butter, melted, plus extra for greasing
Salt and freshly cracked black pepper

Preheat the oven to 200°C/400°F/Gas mark 6. Lightly grease a 12-cup non-stick muffin tin (pan).

Thoroughly wash the kale, remove and discard the entire stalk. Wrap the leaves in a clean kitchen towel to dry, then chop very finely.

Put the kale and the capsicums into a bowl then crumble in the feta cheese. Stir in the onions, garlic and the Parmesan. Add the flour and lightly mix to combine.

Stir in the eggs, milk and butter and gently mix together until all the ingredients are thoroughly combined.

Season with salt and pepper and divide equally between the prepared muffin tin.

Bake for about 15 minutes, or until a skewer, when inserted into the center, comes out clean.

Leave to cool slightly for about 5 minutes before turning out onto a wire rack to go cold.

Note: Substitute the feta with soft goats' cheese, if you like.

Ginger, Carrot and Orange Smoothie

SERVES 2

This is one of my favourite smoothies. I love the taste combination of the ginger and orange with a touch of lime. Together they add a very light and refreshing flavour. I find the ginger especially good for the digestion.

3 stalks of kale
2 medium carrots
1 small knob of fresh ginger
Zest of 1 orange
2 cups (16 fl oz/500 ml)
　　orange juice
Lime juice
1-2 tablespoons honey or
　　agave syrup
Ice cubes

Thoroughly wash the kale, remove and discard the tough lower part of the stalk and roughly chop the leaves.

Peel and chop the carrots and place into a blender with the kale, ginger, orange zest and orange juice.

Add the honey and ice cubes and blend until thick, smooth and creamy.

Add lime juice to taste and adjust the level of sweetness by adding honey or agave syrup to suit your taste.

Serve immediately.

Ham, Zucchini and Cheese Muffins

MAKES 12-15

These muffins are also ideal to prepare if you are catering for vegetarians as well as meat-eaters. Simply prepare the mixture up to the stage where the ham is added, then divide the mixture in half and fold in the ham through one half. Bacon, salami or chorizo sausage can be substituted for the ham, if you like.

Preheat the oven to 180°C/350°F/Gas mark 4. Lightly grease a 12-hole muffin tin (pan).

Thoroughly wash the kale, remove and discard the entire stalk and finely chop the leaves.

Sift the flour into a bowl; add the kale, zucchini, onion, Cheddar and cottage cheese and stir to combine.

Mix in the eggs and oil then season with salt and pepper. Give the mixture a good stir and fold in the ham.

Pour the mixture into the prepared muffins tins and bake for about 20-25 minutes, until golden and cooked through when tested with a skewer.

4 large stalks of kale
1 cup (4 oz/115 g) self-rising (self-raising) flour
12 oz (350 g) zucchini (courgettes), coarsely grated
1 onion, coarsely grated
2/3 1/2 cup (5 1/2 oz/160 g) Cheddar (tasty) cheese, grated
3/4 cup (6 oz/175 g) low-fat cottage cheese (farmers' cheese)
5 eggs, lightly beaten
1/3 cup (2 1/2 fl oz/75 ml) extra light olive oil
Salt and freshly ground pepper
3 oz (90 g) ham, diced

Scrambled Eggs with Kale, Chorizo Sausage and Cottage Cheese

SERVES 4

This dish can be prepared using bacon or minced (ground) beef instead of the chorizo sausage. For a vegetarian option, omit the sausage altogether or substitute with diced potatoes.

Thoroughly wash the kale, remove and discard the thick lower part of the stalk.

Finely chop the leaves and the upper, more tender, part of the stalk and set aside.

Heat the oil in a large non-stick frying pan and fry the chorizo sausages and shallots until the chorizo is golden and the shallots are soft.

Add the kale and continue cooking until it wilts and is cooked, about 5-7 minutes. Stir regularly while cooking.

In a bowl, whisk the eggs, then lightly mix in the cottage cheese. Season with salt and pepper, to taste.

Pour the egg mixture over the kale and cook until the eggs start to set then gently mix with a fork until the eggs are completely mixed in with the other ingredients and have set.

Serve on a thick slice of your favourite toasted bread and with a drizzle of Worcestershire sauce.

6-8 stalks of kale
1-2 tablespoons extra virgin olive oil
2 chorizo sausages, diced
6 shallots/spring onions/ scallions, sliced
8 extra-large eggs
250 g (9 oz) low-fat cottage cheese (farmers' cheese)
Salt and freshly cracked black pepper
Bread, toasted, to serve
Worcestershire sauce (optional)

SOUPS

Chorizo Sausage, Bean and Quinoa Soup

Creamy Corn, Pea and Bacon Soup

Curried Lentil and Kale Soup

Ribolitta Kale Soup

Roasted Capsicum and Vermicelli Noodle Soup

Roasted Pumpkin and Sweet Potato Soup

Chorizo Sausage, Bean and Quinoa Soup

SERVES 6-8

This is a thick and hearty soup perfect for those cold wintery nights and a meal on its own. You can substitute the chorizo sausage with bacon or, if you are a vegetarian, leave out the meat all together. You can also substitute the sausage with chicken, if you prefer.

6 stalks curly kale

1 tablespoon extra virgin olive oil

2-3 chorizo sausages, about 12 oz (340 g) total weight, diced

2 red onions, finely chopped

2 garlic cloves, finely chopped

1 tablespoon tomato paste/purée

2 teaspoons smoked or sweet paprika

2/3 cup (4 oz/115 g) quinoa, rinsed and drained

9 cups (3 3/4 pints/2.1 litres) hot chicken or beef stock

2 bay leaves

Salt and pepper

2 x 14 oz (400 g) cans cannellini beans, rinsed and drained.

Lemon juice, for serving

Thoroughly wash the kale, remove and discard the lower thicker part of the stalk and finely shred the leaves. Set aside.

Heat the oil in a large saucepan and sauté the chorizo and onions until the onion is soft and the chorizo is golden.

Stir in the garlic and cook for about 30 seconds, then stir in the tomato paste and paprika.

Add the quinoa, stock and bay leaves and season with salt and pepper. Bring to the boil, reduce the heat, cover and simmer for 15-18 minutes.

Add the kale and beans, bring to the boil, reduce the heat, cover and simmer for 5-10 minutes, until the kale is tender and the quinoa is fully cooked.

Remove the bay leaf, adjust the seasoning and serve with a good squeeze of lemon juice.

Creamy Corn, Pea and Bacon Soup

This is a very chunky soup. If you prefer your soups less chunky, purée half the soup (the corn and peas with the stock) before you add the kale.

Thoroughly wash the kale, remove and discard the lower thicker part of stalk then finely chop the leaves. Set aside.

In a large saucepan, heat the oil until hot then cook the bacon until crisp. Remove from the pan with a slotted spoon and place on kitchen paper to drain. Set aside.

Add the leek and onion to the saucepan and sauté until soft and just starting to brown slightly. If necessary, add a little more oil.

Stir in the mustard then add the corn, peas and stock, bring to the boil, reduce the heat, cover and simmer for about 15 minutes.

Return the bacon to the soup and stir in the kale, season with salt and a good grind of pepper.

Bring back to the boil, reduce the heat, cover and simmer for about 5-8 minutes until the kale is cooked.

Stir in the cream and leave on the stove on low heat just long enough for the cream to heat through.

Serve with a good grind of freshly cracked black pepper.

6 stalks of cavolo nero (Tuscan kale)

1-2 tablespoons extra virgin olive oil

4½ oz (125 g) streaky bacon, cut into bite sized pieces

1 large leek, washed and sliced

1 brown onion, finely chopped

1-2 teaspoons English mustard

17½ oz (500 g) frozen sweetcorn

17½ oz (500 g) frozen peas

8 cups (3½ pints/2 litres) hot chicken or vegetable stock

Salt and freshly cracked black pepper

½ cup (4 fl oz/125 ml) low-fat (half-fat) cream

Curried Lentil and Kale Soup

SERVES 6-8

This is quite a thick soup as the lentils expand and bulk up quite a bit during cooking. If, once the soup is cooked, you find it is too thick for you, add some extra stock or water.

8 stalks of kale
2 cups (1 lb/450 g) dried red lentils
2 tablespoons extra virgin olive oil
1 large onion, finely chopped
3 large garlic cloves, finely chopped
1 tablespoon freshly grated ginger
1 long red chilli, de-seeded and finely chopped
1 tablespoon curry paste or powder
1 tablespoon ground cumin
1 teaspoon ground coriander
1 tablespoon freshly grated turmeric or 1 teaspoon ground turmeric
9 cups (3 3/4 pints/2.1 litres) hot vegetable stock or water
Salt and freshly ground black pepper
Lemon or lime juice, for serving

Thoroughly wash the kale, remove and discard the thick lower part of the stalk. Finely chop the leaves and the more tender upper part of the stalk, set aside.

Pick over the lentils and remove any dirt and fine grit then wash in a sieve under cold running water until the water runs clear. Drain well.

Heat the oil in a large saucepan and sauté the onion until soft and golden. Add the garlic, ginger and chilli and cook for about 1 minute.

Stir in the curry paste or powder, cumin, coriander and turmeric and cook for another 1 minute stirring regularly so that the spices do not burn.

Add the lentils, pour in the stock or water and bring to the boil. Reduce the heat, cover and simmer for about 20-25, or until the lentils are tender.

Stir in the kale and simmer covered for about 5 minutes, until the kale is cooked.

Serve with a generous squeeze of lemon or lime juice.

Ribolitta Kale Soup

This is a real 'peasant' soup, which evolved from whatever ingredients were on hand and stale bread (which was never thrown away) which was used to add thickness and make the soup more substantial. Traditionally the bread was cut into chunks and stirred into the soup. I prefer to toast it first. The olive oil on the bread as it toasts add richness to the soup.

Thoroughly wash the kale, remove and discard the thick lower part of the stalk.

Finely chop the leaves and the more tender upper part of the stalk, set aside.

Heat the oil in a large saucepan and cook the onion, carrots and celery over medium heat until soft.

Add the garlic, fennel seeds and the thyme leaves and cook for 1–2 minutes until fragrant then stir in the tomato paste and cook for another 1 minute.

Add the kale with the tomatoes, stock, salt and pepper. Bring to the boil, reduce the heat and simmer covered for about 25 minutes.

Using a fork, mash half the beans and stir into the soup with the other half that have been left whole. Cover and simmer for another 10 minutes.

Break the bread into bite-size chunks and stir into the soup. Serve with a generous drizzle of extra virgin olive oil and Parmesan shavings.

Leave the soup to rest for about 10 minutes before serving.

1 small bunch cavolo nero (Tuscan kale)

2-3 tablespoons extra virgin olive oil

1 large red onion, chopped

2 carrots, peeled and finely diced

2 stalks celery, finely diced

4 garlic cloves, chopped

½ teaspoon fennel seeds

3-4 sprigs fresh thyme

1 tablespoon tomato paste

1 x 14 oz (400 g) can diced tomatoes

6 cups (2½ pints/1.5 litres) stock or water

Salt and freshly cracked black pepper

1 x 14 oz (400 g) can cannellini beans, drained

Extra virgin olive oil, for serving

4-6 thick slices stale bread such as pane di casa or ciabatta

Parmesan shavings, for serving

Roasted Capsicum and Vermicelli Noodle Soup

SERVES 6-8

This is one of my favourite soups. I usually use a stick blender to purée my soups I find this method is easy and it certainly cuts down on the washing up.

3 lb 5 oz (1.25 kg) red capsicums (bell peppers)
6 large stalks of kale
2 tablespoons extra virgin olive oil
2 large red onions, peeled and roughly chopped
4 garlic cloves, chopped
1 teaspoon fennel seeds
1 teaspoon sweet paprika
½ –1 teaspoon chilli flakes (optional)
Salt and freshly cracked black pepper
7 cups (3 pints/1.75 litres) hot vegetable or chicken stock
2 nests of thin vermicelli egg noodles, broken into small pieces
Balsamic vinegar, for serving
Grated Parmesan, for serving

Preheat the grill (broiler) and line a large baking sheet with non-stick baking or parchment paper.

Cut the capsicums in half, remove the seeds and membrane then place cut side down on the prepared baking sheet.

Brush the capsicums with a little extra virgin olive oil and grill (broil) until tender and the skin is charred, about 20 minutes.

Remove from the baking sheet and put into a large plastic bag and lightly seal. Leave for about 10 minutes then remove the skin from the peppers.

In the meantime, thoroughly wash the kale, remove the stalks and finely chop the leaves, set aside.

Heat the oil in a large saucepan and cook the onions and garlic until soft. Stir in the fennel seeds, paprika and chilli, if using.

Add the capsicums to the pan, season with salt and pepper and pour in the stock. Bring to the boil, reduce the heat, cover and simmer on low heat for about 20-25 minutes. Remove from the heat and purée the soup, bring back up to the boil, add the kale and noodles and stir well.

Cover, reduce the heat and simmer on low heat for about 8-10 minutes, until kale is tender.

Drizzle balsamic vinegar over the soup before serving with Parmesan.

Roasted Pumpkin and Sweet Potato Soup

SERVES 6-8

The combination of the roasted pumpkin, sweet potato and kale go really well together. A very hearty and satisfying soup, ideal to make for a cold winters night. A meal on its own especially if you add some croutons.

Preheat the oven to 200°C/400°F/Gas mark 6. Line 2 baking sheets with non-stick baking or parchment paper.

Place the squash and potatoes in a single layer on the sheets with the unpeeled and whole garlic cloves. Season with salt and pepper, drizzle with a little extra virgin olive oil and toss well so that they are coated in the oil and seasoning.

Roast in the oven for about 20–30 minutes, or until tender and slightly charred.

Thoroughly wash the kale, remove and discard the thick lower part of the stalk, then chop the leaves very finely into longish strands. Set aside.

Heat the extra tablespoon of oil in a large pan and sauté the onion until soft. Stir in the thyme.

Squeeze the garlic out of its skin and add to the saucepan with the roasted vegetables. Pour in the stock, bring to the boil, reduce the heat, cover and simmer for about 10 minutes.

Purée the soup, add the kale and bring back to the boil, reduce the heat, cover and simmer for 8–10 minutes, until the kale is cooked.

Serve with a dollop of sour cream or yogurt.

- 2¼ lb (1 kg) butternut squash, peeled and cut into small chunks
- 2¼ lb (1 kg) sweet potato (kumera), peeled and cut into small chunks
- 4–5 garlic cloves
- Salt and freshly cracked black pepper
- Extra virgin olive oil, plus 1 tablespoon extra
- 4–6 large stalks of kale
- 1 large onion, chopped
- 6 sprigs thyme
- 8 cups (3½ pints/2 litres) hot chicken or vegetable stock
- Salt and freshly cracked black pepper
- Sour cream or Greek (strained plain) yogurt, for garnish

Note: This is quite a thick soup; if you find it too thick just add extra stock or water. For a vegan option, omit the yogurt and serve garnished with a drizzle of extra virgin olive oil.

SALADS

Asian Salad with Toasted Almonds

Beetroot and Kale Salad

Kale Fattoush Salad

Kale and Quinoa Tabbouleh

Fennel, Orange and Carrot Salad with Ginger Dressing

Kale and Tomato Salad with Tahini Dressing

Kale, Pomegranate and Grapefruit Salad

Kaleslaw with Wasabi Mayonnaise

Mexican Salad

Olive, Tomato and Bocconcini Salad

Pasta and Kale Salad

Potato, Tomato and Olive Salad

Rice Salad

Asian Salad with Toasted Almonds

This salad is ideal served with any roasted or grilled meat, chicken or fish. It is great for a party and the dressing tantalises the tastebuds and leaves you wanting more.

Wash and dry the kale and set aside (a salad spinner is best to use for thoroughly drying the kale).

Using a speed peeler (or standard vegetable peeler) shave the carrots and cucumbers into thin ribbons and place into a large bowl.

Add the kale, radishes, shallots, bean sprouts and as much of the mint and coriander leaves as you like.

Whisk together all the dressing ingredients and pour over the salad starting with a small quantity and adding more according to taste and texture.

Toss the salad well making sure that all the ingredients are coated with the dressing.

Transfer the salad onto a serving platter and serve garnished with the toasted almond flakes.

125 g (4½ oz) baby kale
2 medium carrots, peeled
2 Lebanese cucumbers
10 small radishes, finely sliced
6 shallots/spring onions/scallions, sliced diagonally
2 cups (1 lb/450 g) bean sprouts
½ cup mint leaves, roughly chopped
½ cup coriander (cilantro) leaves, roughly chopped
½ cup (2 oz/60 g) toasted almond flakes

DRESSING

1 tablespoon fish sauce (nam pla)
2 teaspoons palm or brown sugar
Juice of 1 lime
1-2 long red chillies, sliced
1 garlic clove, finely grated
½ teaspoon sesame oil
1 tablespoon olive oil

Note: The dressing is best added just before serving. Check the ingredients in the fish sauce if you are gluten or wheat intolerant.

Beetroot and Kale Salad

SERVES 6-10

This salad is an all-time favourite and looks stunning on a white platter. If you can't find baby kale, use the curly kale. The leaves should be thoroughly washed and the entire thick part of the stalk removed and the leaves chopped.

17½ oz (500 g) fresh beetroot left whole with a small part of the stalk.

4½ oz (125 g) baby kale

½ red capsicum (bell pepper), diced

1 medium-large carrot, coarsely grated (shredded)

1 red onion, halved and sliced

4 shallots/scallions/spring onions, finely sliced

1 x 14 oz (400 g) can cannellini beans, rinsed and drained

DRESSING

1 garlic clove, finely grated

2 tablespoons red wine vinegar

4 tablespoons extra virgin olive oil

Salt and freshly cracked black pepper

Preheat the oven to 180°C/350°F/Gas mark 4.

Scrub the beetroot, leave the skin on and wrap in foil. Bake for about 30-40 minutes, until tender. Leave to cool then peel and dice. Place on kitchen paper and pat dry to remove any excess moisture.

Wash the kale and dry well, using a salad spinner if you have one, and place into a large bowl.

Add the capsicum and carrot and red onion.

Add the onions and the drained beans. Add the diced beetroot.

To make the dressing, mix all the ingredients together. Taste and adjust the seasoning as required. Pour over the salad and toss well.

Transfer the salad to a serving platter and serve.

Note: Home cooked beetroot is best to use and well worth the effort. If you see the canned variety, whole beetroot is better than the slices.

Kale Fattoush Salad

You can serve this salad as a side dish or as a main meal for lunch.

Preheat the oven to 180°C/350°F/Gas mark 4. Line a baking sheet with non-stick baking or parchment paper.

Cut the pita bread into bite-sized chunks, drizzle with a little extra virgin olive oil and season with a little salt. Place onto the prepared baking sheet and bake until crisp and golden, about 12–15 minutes. Leave to cool slightly

Meanwhile, in a bowl, to make the dressing, whisk together the remaining oil, the vinegar, lemon juice and sumac and set aside.

Place the baked bread into a bowl with the cucumbers, tomatoes, onion, radishes and mint.

Add the dressing, season with salt and pepper, mix well and leave for about 5 minutes.

Toss the kale through the salad, check and adjust the seasoning and serve.

3 round pita pocket breads
4 tablespoons extra virgin olive oil
1 tablespoon red wine vinegar
2 tablespoons lemon juice
2 teaspoons sumac seasoning
3 Lebanese cucumbers, halved then thickly sliced
3 tomatoes, halved then cut into wedges
1 red onion, halved and finely sliced
4 radishes, sliced (optional)
2 tablespoons roughly chopped fresh mint
Salt and freshly cracked black pepper
125 g (4½ oz) baby kale, washed and dried

Note: Sumac is a seasoning that is widely used in Middle Eastern cooking and can be found at most delicatessens and green grocers where spices are sold.

Kale and Quinoa Tabouleh

SERVES 6-8

Traditionally tabouleh is made using parsley and cracked (bulgher) wheat. I have added the kale for an even healthier alternative and have used quinoa instead of the cracked wheat to make it suitable for people who have an intolerance to wheat and or gluten.

1 cup (6 oz/175 g) quinoa
   grain, rinsed and
   drained
2 cups (16 fl oz/500 ml)
   water
10-12 stalks cavolo nero
   (Tuscan kale)
½ cup (4 fl oz/125 ml)
   extra virgin olive oil
Juice of 1-2 lemons
Salt and freshly cracked
   black pepper
3 firm, ripe tomatoes, diced
1 red onion, finely chopped
4 shallots/scallions/spring
   onions/sliced
3 Lebanese cucumbers,
   diced
1 cup (large bunch) finely
   chopped flat leaf parsley

Place the quinoa and water into a small saucepan and set over medium heat. Bring to the boil, reduce the heat, cover and simmer for 10 minutes, until all the water is absorbed. Remove from the heat, leave covered for about 10 minutes before fluffing up with a fork, then cool completely.

Thoroughly wash the kale, remove and discard the entire stalk, chop the leaves very finely and place into a large bowl.

Whisk together the oil, lemon juice and salt and pepper and pour one-third of this dressing over the kale. With your fingertips rub the dressing into the kale until it is completely coated.

Add the tomatoes to the kale with the cooled quinoa, both types of onions, cucumbers and parsley, and mix together well.

Pour in the remaining dressing and toss well, taste and adjust the seasoning and amount of lemon juice to taste.

Allow to stand for at least 30 minutes before serving.

Note: This salad needs a fair amount of dressing so that all the flavours of all the ingredients are blended. You can vary the amount to suit your taste.

Fennel, Orange and Carrot Salad with Ginger Dressing

SERVE 6

This is a beautiful delicate tasting salad and ideal to serve with grilled fish or other grilled seafood. I love the mix of the fresh fennel, blood oranges and ginger together, it makes this salad a winner.

125 g (4½ oz) baby kale
2 bulbs baby fennel
2 small blood oranges, plus extra juice (optional)
1 carrot, peeled
1-2 teaspoons fresh ginger, finely grated
1 tablespoon honey
1 tablespoon rice wine vinegar
Salt and freshly cracked black pepper
Extra virgin olive oil

Wash the kale and dry well preferably using a salad spinner, if you have one.

Trim any tough outer leaves from the fennel, if necessary, then cut the vegetable in half and slice finely. Reserve the herby fronds for the garnish.

Peel the oranges and remove all the pith. With a paring knife carefully slice along each side of each orange segment to release the pulp in one piece and remove from the outer skin. Do this over a bowl as you need to collect any juices from the orange.

Using a vegetable peeler slice the carrot into ribbons.

Arrange the kale, fennel, orange segments and carrots on a serving platter.

Whisk together the collected orange juice, ginger, honey and rice wine vinegar, and season with salt and pepper. Add more orange juice if there wasn't enough collected from the segmented oranges. You will need about ½ cup (4 fl oz/125 ml) of orange juice altogether.

Pour the dressing over the salad, then drizzle lightly with some extra virgin olive oil and garnish with the green leafy fronds from the fennel.

Note: If baby kale is not available you can use cavolo nero (Tuscan kale). Thoroughly wash the kale and remove the entire stalks. Cut the leaves into smallish pieces, coat with a little of the dressing and lightly rub with your fingertips so that the dressing softens the kale. Then follow recipe as above.

Kale and Tomato Salad with Tahini Dressing

This salad is great as an accompaniment to a piece of fish, meat or chicken and is delicious in a wrap. Any leftover dressing will keep for quite a few days, covered, in the refrigerator.

Wash the kale and dry thoroughly, using a salad spinner if you have one.

Halve the tomatoes and place into a large bowl with the kale, onion slices and olives.

To make the dressing, whisk all the ingredients together in a small bowl, adding the lesser amount of lemon juice to begin with. If you find the dressing is too thick, just add a little extra water. Taste and adjust the seasoning and lemon juice as you go. Pour as much, or as little, over the salad as you like. Toss well to combine.

125 g (4½ oz) baby kale
450 g (1 lb) grape tomatoes
1 large red onion, halved and sliced
½ cup (3 oz/90 g) black Kalamata olives, pitted

DRESSING
¼ cup (2 fl oz/60 ml) tahini paste
1 small garlic clove, very finely grated or pound in a mortar and pestle
½ cup (4 fl oz/125 ml) water
2-3 tablespoons lemon juice
½ teaspoon ground cumin
1-2 tablespoons extra virgin olive oil
Salt and freshly cracked black pepper

Note: If your jar of tahini paste has been sitting in the pantry for a while, make sure that you stir it well before using. The oil in the tahini paste has a tendency to separate from the tahini pulp if it left.

Kale, Pomegranate and Grapefruit Salad

There are only a few ingredients in this salad yet the results are stunning, not only to the eye but to the tastebuds as well. The juicy pomegranate seeds sprinkled all over this salad make it really stand out. Lovely with roasted meat such as pork.

In a bowl, mix all the dressing ingredients together and set aside for the flavours to develop. Remove and discard the garlic just before using the dressing.

Wash the kale and dry thoroughly, using a salad spinner if you have one. Place the kale onto a large serving platter and scatter the slices of onion over the top.

Peel the grapefruit and remove all the white pith. Using a paring knife, carefully cut out the flesh from between each segment membrane. It is best to do this over a bowl so that you can collect any juices as you work.

Pour any juices collected into the dressing mixture.

Arrange the grapefruit segments over the kale and onion.

To remove the seeds from the pomegranate, cut the fruit in half and using the back of a wooden spoon, bash each half over the salad to release the seeds. Garnish the salad with shavings of Parmesan. Just before serving, scatter the pomegranate seeds over the top and drizzle over the dressing.

115 g (4 oz) baby kale
1 small red onion, finely sliced into rings
2 ruby red grapefruit
1 large pomegranate
Parmesan shavings

DRESSING

2-3 tablespoons extra virgin olive oil
2 tablespoons lemon juice
1-2 teaspoons Dijon mustard
1 garlic clove, peeled, lightly smashed and left whole
1 teaspoon honey
Salt and freshly cracked black pepper
1 tablespoon chives, finely chopped

Note: The juices from the pomegranate will splatter all over the salad when you use the method above to release the seeds. I think this adds to the look and the taste of the salad. If you would rather have a 'neater' look, release the seeds over a bowl and drizzle any juices collected over the salad.

Kaleslaw with Wasabi Mayonnaise

SERVES 6-8

I prefer using the cavolo nero (Tuscan kale) for this recipe as the leaves are generally softer. You can, however, use curly kale for this recipe if you prefer.

1 bunch cavolo nero
(Tuscan kale)
1 tablespoon red wine
vinegar
2 medium carrots, coarsely
grated
1 red onion, halved and
finely sliced
2 stalks celery, finely sliced
6 shallots, finely sliced
1-2 long red chillies, de-
seeded and sliced
Salt and freshly cracked
black pepper
½ cup (4 fl oz/125 ml)
mayonnaise
1-2 tablespoons extra virgin
olive oil
2 teaspoons soy sauce
2-3 tablespoons wasabi
paste

Thoroughly wash the kale, remove and discard most of the lower thick part of the stalk and finely shred the leaves.

Place the kale into a bowl and pour in the red wine vinegar. Using your fingertips rub the vinegar into the kale. This helps to soften the kale.

Add the carrots, onion, celery, shallots and chilli, then season with salt and pepper and mix well to combine.

Mix together the mayonnaise, oil, soy sauce and as much wasabi paste as you like.

Pour over the salad and mix really well with your hands.

Cover and chill for 1-2 hours before serving if possible.

Note: You can add as much or as little wasabi paste as you like. It is best to start with a lower amount and add more after tasting, a little at a time, until you reach a taste that you like.

Mexican Salad

If you are looking for a colourful and very tasty salad to make for, or take to, a BBQ, then this is it. Not only does it go really well with any barbecued meat, it is perfect for any vegetarian that you may also have to cater for.

To make the dressing, whisk all the ingredients together in a small bowl.

Thoroughly wash the kale. Tear the large leaves into small pieces and discard the entire stalk. Dry the leaves by either wrapping in a clean kitchen towel or using a salad spinner.

Place the kale leaves into a large bowl and pour in most of the dressing. With your hands, rub the dressing into the kale. You will feel the kale starting to soften. Set aside to continue softening while you prepare the other ingredients.

Dry fry the corn in a non-stick frying pan until it turns golden. Keep tossing the corn while it is cooking so that it doesn't burn. Remove from the heat and leave to cool.

Add the cool corn, red and green capsicums, onion, onions and red kidney beans to the kale with the remaining dressing, and mix well.

Set the salad aside to absorb all the flavours for at least 30 minutes before arranging on a serving platter.

Note: If you prefer, you can blanche the kale leaves in boiling water for 1-2 minutes only. Drain and refresh in ice cold water to stop the cooking process. Drain well.

1 small bunch purple kale
2 cups (12 oz/350 g) frozen sweet corn kernels, thawed
½ large red capsicum (bell pepper), diced into small pieces
½ large green capsicum (bell pepper), diced into small pieces
1 small red onion, finely chopped
4 shallots/spring onions/ scallions, sliced
14 oz (400 g) can red kidney beans, rinsed and drained

DRESSING

½ teaspoon dried ground oregano
½ teaspoon ground cumin
½ teaspoon paprika
Fresh chilli, finely chopped, to taste
Juice of 1 lime
4 tablespoons extra virgin olive oil
Salt, to taste
Freshly ground black pepper

Olive, Tomato and Bocconcini Salad

SERVES 6

Fresh, colourful and inviting, this salad contains intense and flavourful ingredients that make them a winning combination.

1 bunch cavolo nero
    (Tuscan kale)
3-4 ripe but firm tomatoes
1 cup (6 oz/175 g) green
    olives
4 shallots/spring onion/
    scallions, sliced
2 tablespoons capers
8 oz (225 g) bocconcini
Anchovy fillets (optional)

DRESSING
1 garlic clove
2 teaspoons honey
2 teaspoons Dijon mustard
1 tablespoon lemon juice
1 teaspoon red wine
    vinegar
4 tablespoons extra virgin
    olive oil
Salt and freshly cracked
    black pepper

To make the dressing, pound the garlic with a little salt in a mortar and pestle until it is a very fine purée. Mix in the remaining ingredients, taste and adjust the seasoning to taste.

Thoroughly wash the kale, remove most of the thick stalks and dry the leaves well, using a salad spinner if you have one.

Tear the kale leaves and place into a bowl. Pour a little of the dressing over the leaves and, using your hands, gently rub the dressing and the leaves together.

Arrange the kale on a serving platter. Cut the tomatoes into wedges and arrange over the kale with the olives, onions and capers.

Tear the bocconcini into bite-size pieces and scatter over the salad with the anchovies, if using. Drizzle the remaining dressing over the salad and serve.

Note: Choose kale that has small young tender leaves for this recipe. Baby kale can be substituted for the cavolo nero. Curly kale can also be used; you will need about 8-10 stalks depending on size and you will need to remove almost the entire stalk and tear the leaves into small leaves.

Pasta and Kale Salad

A great salad to feed a crowd on any occasion. A real taste of the Mediterranean in a bowl and a salad that would complement any other food on the table. Ideal for vegetarians.

Cook the pasta in lots of salted boiling water until *al dente*, or according to the packet instructions, drain and rinse under cold running water to stop the cooking process, drain again and set aside.

Thoroughly wash the kale, remove and discard the entire stalk and chop the leaves into fine strips. Use a salad spinner, if you have one, or wrap the kale in a clean kitchen towel to remove any excess moisture and dry.

Cut the artichoke heart into quarters and slice the capsicums and tomatoes into strips.

Place the pasta, kale, artichokes, capsicums, sun-dried tomatoes and olives into a large bowl. Add the capers, shallots and parsley and toss well.

In a bowl, whisk together the oil, vinegar, and salt and pepper. Pour the dressing over the salad and toss well. Check and adjust the seasoning and the amount of dressing.

Leave the salad to stand for about 30 minutes for all the flavours to develop before arranging on a serving platter.

8 oz (225 g) small pasta of your choice

6 large stalks of cavolo nero (Tuscan kale)

9 oz (250 g) jar artichoke hearts, drained

9 oz (250 g) jar char-grilled capsicums (bell peppers), drained

3 oz (90 g) semi-dried tomatoes

1 cup (6 oz/175 g) Kalamata olives, pitted

1 tablespoon capers, drained (optional)

4-6 shallots/spring onions/scallions, finely sliced

½ cup (bunch) flat leaf parsley, finely chopped

4-5 tablespoons extra virgin olive oil

1-2 tablespoons balsamic vinegar

Salt and freshly cracked black pepper

Potato, Tomato and Olive Salad

SERVES 6-8

One of my favourite salads and my version of a potato salad without any heavy creamy dressing. Always popular and I always tend to make it when I need to make a few salads for a get together.

4 oz (115 g) baby kale
2¼ lb (1 kg) baby (chat) potatoes, washed and halved
⅓ cup (2½ fl oz/75 ml) extra virgin olive oil
1-2 tablespoons red wine vinegar
Salt and freshly cracked black pepper
1 lb 2 oz (500 g) red grape or cherry tomatoes, halved
1 red onion, peeled, halved and thinly sliced
1 cup (6 oz/175 g) Kalamata olives, pitted
½ cup (bunch) flat leaf parsley leaves, roughly chopped

Wash the kale and dry thoroughly, using a salad spinner, if you have one. Set aside.

Boil or steam the potatoes until tender.

To make the dressing, whisk together the oil, vinegar, and salt and pepper.

Drain the potatoes well and while still warm, place them in a large bowl and mix in most of the dressing. Set aside for the potatoes to absorb the dressing for about 15 minutes. (Potatoes absorb dressing much better whilst still warm.)

Add the tomatoes, onion slices and olives to the potatoes with the remaining dressing and toss well to combine. Check and adjust the seasoning and dressing, adding more oil or vinegar according to taste. Just before serving toss in the kale and place on a serving platter. Serve at room temperature.

Note: You can substitute cavolo nero (Tuscan kale) for baby kale, if you like. If you do, use the leaves and discard the entire stalk. After washing, chop the leaves into thin strips and mix into the salad at the same time as the other ingredients.

Rice Salad

This is quite a large salad; great for large families or for feeding a crowd. Because it is a so large it requires a fair amount of dressing. You may need to adjust the quantity of the dressing to suit your taste.

Thoroughly wash the kale. Remove and discard the entire stalk and chop the leaves very finely. Set aside.

Place the rice into a large bowl with the kale, capsicum, peas, carrots, corn and dill.

Slice the olives or leave whole, if you prefer, and add to the bowl with the vegetables.

To make the dressing, in a small bowl, whisk together the oil, vinegar, lemon juice, and salt and pepper.
Pour over the rice and mix well. Check and adjust the seasoning and also the amount of dressing.

If possible leave the salad to develop for 1-2 hours before serving.

6-8 stalks cavolo nero (Tuscan kale)

3 cups (1 lb 6 oz/600 g) cold cooked rice

1 large red capsicum (red pepper), diced into small pieces

2 cups (8 oz/225 g) cooked peas

2 medium carrots, coarsely grated

2 cups (12 oz/350 g) cooked sweet corn kernels

3 tablespoons fresh dill, chopped

½ cup (3 oz/90 g) stuffed green olives

4-5 tablespoons extra virgin olive oil

2 tablespoons red wine vinegar

2-3 tablespoons lemon juice

Salt and freshly cracked black pepper

VEGETARIAN

Beetroot and Kale Risotto with Feta Cheese

Kale-elloni

Kale Chips

Kale Pasta

Kale Pesto

Kale, Leek and Feta Cheese Frittata

Kale, Olive and Cheese Filo Rolls

Kale, Quinoa and Tomato Flans

Lentils with Tomato and Kale

Potato Croquettes

Pasta with Zucchini, Roasted Pumpkin and Kale

Potato, Kale and Chickpea Curry

Ratatouille

Roasted Sweet Potato and Tomato Frittata

Spiced Red Lentils

Tomato, Mushroom and Chickpea Curry

Vegetable and Coconut Curry

Curried Kale with Black Beans

Beetroot and Kale Risotto with Feta Cheese

SERVES 4-6

I prefer my risotto to be really soft and almost porridge-like. This usually means cooking it for about 30 minutes, if you run out of stock and the risotto is still not quite cooked to the way you like it, you can add some extra hot water. Fresh ricotta cheese can be substituted for the goats' cheese.

Thoroughly wash the kale. Remove and discard the entire thick part of the stalk and finely chop the leaves. Set aside.

Heat the oil in a large saucepan, add the onion and fry gently until soft. Stir in the garlic and cook for about 30 seconds until fragrant.

Stir the rice into the onion and garlic mixture and cook until the rice turns opaque. Pour in the wine and keep stirring until it is absorbed.

Stir the beetroot and any of its juices into the rice, season well with salt and pepper and cook for about 1 minute.

In another saucepan, heat the stock until hot and leave on a low simmer on the stove throughout the cooking time.

Add one ladleful of stock to the rice and stir continuously until it is absorbed. Continue doing this one ladleful at a time until there is just over a ladleful of stock left. At this stage the rice should be almost cooked.

Stir in the kale and continue cooking for another 4–5 minutes, slowly adding the stock until the rice is fully cooked and the kale is tender.

Stir in the butter, Parmesan and crumbled cheese, check and adjust the seasoning and serve immediately, garnished with some extra crumbled goats' cheese.

8 large stalks of cavolo nero (Tuscan kale)

2 tablespoons olive oil

1 red onion, finely chopped

4 garlic cloves, finely chopped

2 cups (14 oz/400 g) arborio rice

½ cup (4 fl oz/125 ml) white wine

1 lb (450 g) fresh beetroot, peeled and coarsely grated (shredded)

Salt and freshly cracked black pepper

6½ –7 cups (about 3 pints) vegetable stock

1 tablespoon butter

½ cup (1½ oz/45 g) Parmesan, freshly grated

3 oz (90 g) feta cheese, crumbled

Soft goats' cheese, for serving

Kale-elloni

SERVES 4-6

These kale-elloni (kale and ricotta cheese-filled cannelloni) are made using a pasta dough made with kale and a filling made with kale and ricotta cheese, topped with a rich tomato sauce. They may take just a little bit of time to make but are worth it and oh so much healthier for you.

CANNELLONI

10 large stalks of kale
2 tablespoons extra virgin olive oil
1 onion, finely chopped
Salt and freshly cracked black pepper
375 g (13 oz) low-fat ricotta
2 tablespoons Parmesan, grated, plus extra to serve
Nutmeg
Half quantity kale pasta, see page 83

To make the cannelloni, thoroughly wash the kale. Remove and discard the thick lower part of the stalk. Finely chop the leaves and the upper, more tender, part of the stalk, set aside.

Heat the oil in a large frying pan and sauté the onion until soft and golden. Add the kale, season with salt and pepper, and continue cooking until the kale is tender and has wilted, about 4–5 minutes. Remove from the heat and allow to cool.

Place the kale and onion mixture in a large bowl and mix in the ricotta, Parmesan and a grating of nutmeg. Check and adjust seasoning.

Roll out the pasta dough into long sheets and cut into pieces 6 x 5 in (16 x 12 cm). You will get 8–12 pieces depending on the thickness of the dough. It is better if the pasta sheets are rolled thin.

Preheat the oven to 200°C/400°F/Gas mark 6.

Arrange the pasta sheets on the work surface and divide the filling evenly between them. Place the filling in a pile along the shorter end of each sheet and roll up into a tube.

To make the sauce, heat the oil in a saucepan and sauté the onion and garlic until soft. Stir in the tomato paste and sugar, and cook for about 1 minute. Stir in the oregano, pour in the passata and water, and season with salt and pepper to taste. Bring to the boil, reduce the heat, cover leaving the lid slightly ajar and simmer for about 7–10 minutes.

Cover the base of a baking dish with half the sauce and place the kale-elloni, seam side down in a single layer on top.

Pour the remaining sauce over the top and scatter with the extra Parmesan. Bake for about 25–30 minutes until cooked and golden on top.

Serve hot with extra Parmesan sprinkled on top.

SAUCE

2 tablespoons extra virgin olive oil

1 small onion, finely chopped

2–3 garlic cloves, finely chopped

2 tablespoons tomato paste

1 teaspoon sugar

½–1 teaspoon dried oregano

24 oz (700 g) jar passata sauce

2 cups (16 fl oz/500 ml) water

Salt and freshly cracked black pepper

Note: Depending on appetite, serving 2 or 3 tubes per person.

Kale Chips

These chips are really delicious and very moreish with whatever flavouring you choose. Kale chips can be stored in an airtight container and will remain fresh and crispy for up to 2-4 days.

1 bunch kale
Extra virgin olive oil
Sea salt

FLAVOURINGS
Chilli flakes
Smoked paprika
Cumin seeds or ground
   cumin
Balsamic vinegar and sea
   salt
Curry power
Chilli and lime zest
A sprinkle of soy sauce
Flavoured salt such as
   garlic or celery

Preheat the oven to 150°C/300°F/Gas mark 2. Line 2-3 baking sheets with non-stick baking or parchment paper.

Remove the kale leaves from the stem, and wash and gently pat the leaves dry. Use a salad spinner, if you have one.

Place the kale leaves into a large bowl with the oil and sea salt and any other flavouring if used and toss until well coated.

Spread onto the prepared baking sheets without overcrowding them or they will not crisp up.

Place in the oven and bake for about 25 minutes. After 10 minutes turn them over, (at this stage they will not be very crispy) and bake for another 10-15 minutes until they are thin and very crispy.

Kale Pasta

SERVES 4

If you are gluten/wheat intolerant, this recipe works using quinoa flour, which is totally gluten/wheat free. Just bear in mind that it may take a little longer in the food processor for the dough to come together into a ball and you may need to add a little more flour

Thoroughly wash the kale, remove and discard the entire stalk then plunge the leaves into a pan of boiling water and cook for 3-4 minutes. Drain and refresh under cold water. Drain again and squeeze out as much of the moisture as you can, then chop finely.

Put the kale into the bowl of a food processor and process to chop again, add the flour and process until the flour and kale have combined and the kale is fine.

Add the eggs and continue processing until the dough comes together into a ball. Pulse a few times: you may need to divide the dough once it comes together and process it in batches to ensure that the kale is completely incorporated and finely chopped into the dough.

Tip the dough out onto a lightly floured surface and knead with your hands for 2-3 minutes.

Wrap in cling film (plastic wrap) and refrigerate for 1 hour before rolling out and shaping in a pasta machine. Alternatively, roll out the dough into a thin rectangle, tidy the edges and cut into thin stands for spaghetti or a little wider for fettuccine. If the dough feels a little sticky it is probably because there was a little too much moisture left in the kale. Just add a little more flour when processing

Cook the pasta in a large pan of salted boiling water to your preferred *al dente* stage.

8-10 stalks cavolo nero (Tuscan kale)
17½ oz (500 g) 00 super fine Italian flour
5 extra-large eggs

Note: I find that the cavolo nero (Tuscan kale) works best in this recipe.

Kale Pesto

MAKES ABOUT 2 CUPS (16 FL OZ/500 ML)

I find the cavolo nero (Tuscan kale) works best for making the pesto. Use this pesto to serve with pasta or over rice or cooked quinoa. Pesto will keep, covered, in the refrigerator for 2-3 days.

10-12 large stalks cavolo nero (Tuscan kale)
Small handful fresh basil leaves including the stalks
3-4 garlic cloves, chopped
4½ oz (125 g) pine nuts
½ -¾ cup (1½ -2 oz/45-60 g) Parmesan, freshly grated
Juice of ½ -1 lemon
⅔- ¾ cup (5-6 fl oz/150-175ml) extra virgin olive oil
Salt and freshly cracked black pepper, to taste

Thoroughly wash the kale. Remove and discard the entire stalk and roughly chop the leaves.

Place the kale, basil, garlic, pine nuts, cheese and lemon juice into a food processor and process until the ingredients are all combined and finely chopped.

With the motor running slowly drizzle in the olive oil starting with the lesser amount until the pesto is a smooth and creamy consistency. Scrape down the sides of the bowl regularly during processing.

Season to taste; add more cheese, oil or lemon juice according to your taste.

Kale, Leek and Feta Cheese Frittata

SERVES 4

This is one of those really quick-and-easy to prepare nourishing meals. Ideal for something quick to eat after work or for lunch when unexpected visitors drop in. A simple salad served with it is great, as is some crusty bread.

Thoroughly wash the kale. Remove and discard the entire stalk and finely chop the leaves. Set aside.

Heat the oil in a medium non-stick frying pan and cook the leek until it softens and starts to take on some colour. Stir in the garlic and cook for a few seconds.

Add the kale, sprinkle with a little salt and cook on medium heat, stirring regularly, for about 5 minutes, until the kale collapses and it is tender.

In the meantime, whisk the eggs with the cream, pepper and salt, if using (keep in mind that feta can be salty).

Preheat the grill (broiler) to medium-hot.

Pour the egg mixture over the kale mixture in the frying pan and gently mix through to combine. Cook on low-medium heat until the frittata is almost set but still runny on the top.

Crumble the cheese and as many slices of chilli as you like over the top, then place the frying pan under the preheated grill and cook until the frittata is set and lightly golden.

Allow to rest for 2–3 minutes before loosening with a spatula and sliding on to a serving dish. Slice and serve garnished with fresh chives.

1 small bunch kale, (8–10 stalks)
1 large leek, thoroughly washed and thinly sliced
2 garlic cloves, finely chopped
2 tablespoons extra virgin olive oil
10 extra-large eggs
½ cup (4 fl oz/125 ml) low-fat cream
Freshly cracked black pepper
Salt (optional)
3 oz (90 g) feta cheese, crumbled
1 long red chilli, finely sliced
Chives, for garnish

Note: Goats' cheese can be substituted for the feta cheese, if you prefer.

Kale, Olive and Cheese Filo Rolls

MAKES 12 ROLLS

These kale and cheese rolls can be frozen and baked as required. They keep for weeks in the freezer and are great to have on hand. To freeze, prepare as above but do not brush with butter or sprinkle with sesame seeds until just before baking. They can be baked from frozen but you may need to bake them for a little longer.

1 bunch kale, about 10–12 large leaves
2–3 tablespoons extra virgin olive oil
1 onion, finely chopped
8 shallots/spring onions/ scallions, chopped
5 oz (150 g) feta cheese, coarsely grated
13 oz (375 g) ricotta
2 tablespoons Parmesan, grated
1/2–3/4 cup (3–4 1/2 oz/ 90–125 g) Kalamata olives, pitted and chopped
2 eggs, lightly beaten
Freshly ground black pepper
12 sheets filo pastry
Extra virgin olive oil, for brushing
1–2 tablespoons butter, melted
Sesame seeds

Thoroughly wash the kale. Remove and discard the thick lower part of the stalk and finely chop the leaves.

Heat the oil in a large frying pan; add the onion and shallots and sauté until soft and lightly golden.

Add the kale and cook on medium-high for 5–8 minutes, until the kale has wilted and is soft. Keep tossing and mixing the kale while cooking. Remove from the heat, place in a bowl and set aside to cool.

Preheat the oven to 200°C/400°F/Gas mark 6. Line a baking sheet with non-stick baking or parchment paper.

Add the feta, ricotta, Parmesan, olives and eggs to the cool kale mixture and season with pepper. Mix well. Taste and add a little salt, if necessary. Divide into 12 portions.

Brush a sheet of filo pastry lightly all over with a little oil then fold in half. Lightly brush one side with oil again and place a portion of the kale filling along one edge.

Fold the pastry over the filling, tuck in the sides then roll into a long roll, making sure the sides are always tucked in as you roll.

Brush the end of the roll with a little oil to seal and place onto the prepared sheet. Repeat with each of the remaining filo sheets and filling.

Brush each roll with melted butter, sprinkle with sesame seeds, then bake for about 25 minutes, until the pastry is golden and crisp.

Kale, Quinoa and Tomato Mini Flans

MAKES 8

These tarts are just as nice eaten cold so are handy for taking to work, picnics and great for school lunches. For the non-vegetarians, diced bacon, pancetta or even chorizo sausage go really well in these tarts. Just add and cook with the shallots before adding the kale.

Place the red quinoa into a small pan with the water, bring to the boil, reduce the heat, cover and simmer for 12–15 minutes, until the quinoa is cooked and all the water is absorbed. Remove from the heat and leave to stand, covered, for about 10 minutes until needed.

Preheat the oven to 180°C/350°F/Gas mark 4. Lightly grease eight 5 in (12 cm) tart tins without a removable base.

Thoroughly wash the kale. Remove and discard the thick lower part of the stalks. Finely chop the leaves and the more tender upper part of the stalks and set aside.

Heat the oil in a large frying pan and sauté the shallots for 2–3 minutes until soft and lightly golden. Add the kale and cook for about 5 minutes, stirring regularly until the kale collapses. Set aside to cool a little.

Whisk together the eggs and milk. Slowly incorporate the flour into the egg mixture then stir in the cheese and the quinoa. Season with salt and pepper to taste.

Stir the kale into the egg and cheese mixture, then pour into the prepared tins and decorate with the tomato halves.

Bake for about 25–30 minutes, until the tarts have set and are golden.

Serve with salad or vegetables.

½ cup (3 oz/90 g) red quinoa, rinsed and drained

1 cup (8 fl oz/250 ml) water

10–12 stalks of cavolo nero (Tuscan kale)

2 tablespoons extra virgin olive oil

4–6 shallots/spring onions/ scallions, sliced

6 extra-large eggs

1¼ cups (10 fl oz/300 ml) low-fat (semi-skimmed) milk

⅔ cup (2¾ oz/80 g) quinoa flour

¾ cup (6 oz/175 g) Cheddar (tasty) cheese, grated

Salt and freshly cracked black pepper

12–18 grape or cherry tomatoes, halved

Lentils with Tomatoes and Kale

SERVES 4

This dish can be served on its own or over some cooked quinoa or rice.

8-10 large stalks kale
2 tablespoons extra virgin
    olive oil
1 large onion, chopped
3 garlic cloves, chopped
1½ tablespoons ground
    cumin
1 tablespoons ground
    coriander
1 knob of fresh turmeric,
    grated, or 2 teaspoons
    ground turmeric
1-2 long red chillies, de-
    seeded and chopped
14 oz (400 g) can diced
    tomatoes
2 x 14 oz (400 g) cans
    lentils, undrained
½ cup (4 fl oz/125 ml)
    water
Salt, to taste
½ cup (small bunch)
    chopped fresh coriander
    (cilantro)
Unsweetened Greek
    (strained plain) yogurt,
    for serving
Lemon juice

Thoroughly wash the kale. Remove and discard the lower thick part of the stalk. Finely chop the leaves and the more tender upper part of the stalk, set aside.

Heat the oil in a large deep frying pan and sauté the onion until soft and lightly browned.

Stir in the garlic and cook for about 30 seconds, until fragrant. Take the pan off the heat and stir in the cumin, coriander, turmeric and chilli. Add a little more oil to the pan if necessary.

Return the pan to the heat and cook the spices for about 1 minute, stirring constantly, so that the spices don't burn.

Add the tomatoes, lentils, water, and season with salt, then bring to the boil. Add the kale, reduce the heat, cover and simmer for about 10 minutes.

Stir in the coriander and simmer uncovered for another 2-3 minutes, until the kale is fully cooked.

Serve with lemon juice stirred through and a dollop of yogurt.

Potato Croquettes

MAKES ABOUT 20

For non-vegetarians, add chopped bacon or prosciutto to the croquettes. Just chop into small pieces and add to the kale while it is cooking with the shallots and garlic.

2¼ lb (1 kg) potatoes
4 large stalks of kale
2 tablespoons extra virgin olive oil
4 shallots/spring onions/ scallions, finely chopped
2 garlic cloves, finely chopped
salt and freshly ground black pepper
pinch of freshly grated nutmeg (optional)
½ cup (2 oz/60 g) flour
2–3 extra-large eggs, beaten
2 cups (4 oz/115 g) panko breadcrumbs
Oil, for shallow frying

Scrub the potatoes, then boil them in their skin until tender. Remove from the heat and set aside until cool enough to handle. Peel and mash the potatoes while still warm.

Meanwhile, thoroughly wash the kale. Remove and discard the entire stalk. Finely chop the leaves and set aside.

Heat the oil in a medium frying pan and sauté the shallots until soft. Stir in the garlic and cook for about 30 seconds.

Add the kale and cook over medium heat for about 5 minutes, until tender. Stir the kale regularly during cooking; it will almost halve in volume.

Place the potatoes into a bowl; add the kale and season with salt and a good grind of black pepper. Add the nutmeg, if using, then mix together until thoroughly combined.

Shape the mixture into longish shaped croquettes. Dust each one with a little flour, dip into the beaten egg, then coat well in the breadcrumbs.

Heat the oil in a large frying pan set over medium heat until hot, and cook the croquettes until golden all over.

Remove from the pan with a slotted spoon and place on kitchen paper to drain off any excess oil.

Pasta with Zucchini, Roasted Pumpkin and Kale

SERVES 6

This dish was created especially for my vegetarian daughters. It has been a family favourite for years and even the non-vegetarians in the family love it. Garlic bread is the only other thing I serve with it.

Preheat the oven to 200°C/400°F/Gas mark 4. Line a baking sheet with non-stick baking or parchment paper.

Peel and cut the pumpkin into cubes, drizzle with 1-2 tablespoons extra virgin olive oil and season with salt and pepper. Place on the prepared sheet and roast in the oven until tender and slightly charred but not overcooked, 20-30 minutes.

Thoroughly wash the kale, remove and discard the thick lower part of the stalk. Chop the leaves and set aside.

Heat the remaining oil in a large frying pan and fry the zucchini until golden on both sides.

In the meantime, bring a large pan of salted water to a rapid boil and cook the pasta, according to the packet instructions, until *al dente*.

Add the kale to the zucchini and continue cooking until the kale collapses, about 3-4 minutes. Stir in the garlic and cook until fragrant.

Combine the pumpkin with the zucchini and kale.

Drain the pasta and reserve some of the cooking liquid. Add the pasta straight into the frying pan and mix with the vegetables and a little of the reserved pasta liquid and continue cooking for a few more minutes until the pasta fully cooks and all the flavours have combined.

Season to taste and serve with plenty of Parmesan scattered on top.

2¼ lb (1 kg) butternut squash
3-5 tablespoons extra virgin olive oil
Salt and freshly cracked black pepper
10-12 stalks of cavolo nero (Tuscan kale)
3 medium zucchini (courgettes), thickly sliced
10½ oz (300 g) pasta of your choice
3 garlic cloves, grated
Salt and freshly cracked black pepper
Parmesan, grated

Potato, Kale and Chickpea Curry

SERVES 6

Pandang leaves are used in Asian cooking to add fragrance to food. Like fresh curry leaves they are available at most Asian grocery shops.

Thoroughly wash the kale. Remove and discard the lower thick part of the stalk. Tear the leaves and the upper more tender part of the stalk into small pieces. Set aside.

Peel and cut the potato and sweet potato into small chunks and set aside.

Heat the oil in a deep pan with a wide cooking surface area and cook the onion until soft.

Add the garlic, chilli, ginger and cook for 1–2 minutes, until fragrant.

Stir in the curry leaves, coriander stalks (use the leaves for the garnish) and curry paste or powder and cook for another 1 minute.

Add the potatoes to the pan with the undrained chickpeas, pandang leaves and stock or water, then season with salt and pepper to taste. Simmer covered for about 15–20 minutes until the potatoes are almost cooked.

Stir in the kale, cover and simmer for about 5 minutes, until the kale is tender.

Sprinkle with lime juice and serve garnished with fresh coriander leaves and sliced chillies.

6–8 large stalks of curly kale

17½ oz (500 g) potatoes

2¼ lb (1 kg) orange sweet potato (kumera)

2 tablespoons olive oil

1 onion, chopped

3 garlic cloves, finely chopped

1–2 long red chillies, de-seeded and sliced, plus extra to serve

2 tablespoons ginger, finely chopped

1 small handful curry leaves

½ cup (bunch) fresh coriander (cilantro) stalks, chopped

2 tablespoons of your favourite curry paste or powder

2 x 14 oz (400 g) cans chickpeas, undrained

2 pan dang leaves (optional)

1½ cups (12 fl oz/375 ml) vegetable stock or water

Salt and pepper

Lime juice

Fresh coriander (cilantro) leaves, for garnish

Ratatouille

SERVES 4-6

This dish tastes lovely hot or served cold; just drizzle with a little extra virgin olive oil before serving.

1 large eggplant (aubergine), cut into cubes

1 green capsicum (bell pepper), seeds removed and cut into cubes

1 red capsicum (bell pepper), seeds removed and cut into cubes

1-2 tablespoons extra virgin olive oil, plus 2 tablespoons extra

Salt and pepper

8 kale stalks

1 large onion, halved and thinly sliced

3 garlic cloves, chopped

14 oz (400 g) can diced tomatoes, undrained

2 carrots, thickly sliced

1 potato, peeled and cubed

3 zucchini (courgettes), thickly sliced

3/4 -1 cup (6-8 fl oz/175-250 ml) water

Preheat the oven to 200°C/400°F/Gas mark 6. Line a large baking sheet with non-stick baking or parchment paper.

Place the eggplant and capsicums in a bowl, drizzle with some extra virgin olive oil and season with salt and pepper and place onto the sheet.

Roast in the oven for about 30 minutes, until tender and slightly charred. Turn the vegetables over once or twice during cooking.

In the meantime, thoroughly wash the kale, remove and discard the thick lower stalks of the kale. Chop the leaves and the upper more tender part of the stalk and set aside.

Heat the extra oil in a large saucepan and sauté the onion until soft and golden. Stir in the garlic and cook until fragrant.

Add the tomatoes, carrots, potato, zucchini and kale. Season with salt and pepper and pour in the water.

Bring to the boil, reduce the heat and gently simmer for 15-20 minutes, until the potatoes and carrots are tender and cooked.

Stir in the roasted eggplant and capsicum, and cook for another 3-5 minutes, until heated through.

Serve as a vegetarian dish with cooked quinoa or rice, or as a side dish with fish, meat or chicken.

Roasted Sweet Potato and Tomato Frittata

SERVES 4

This frittata is delicious eaten cold as well as warm; it's great for a picnic.

Preheat the oven to 200C°/400°F/Gas mark 6. Line a baking sheet with non-stick baking or parchment paper. Peel and cut the potatoes into chunks, coat with a little extra virgin olive oil and roast for about 20 minutes, until tender. Remove from the oven and set aside.

Thoroughly wash the kale, remove and discard the thick lower part of the stalk. Slice the leaves very thinly and set aside.

Heat the oil in a medium non-stick frying pan and lightly cook the tomatoes until they start to soften and the skin starts to blister. Remove from the pan and set aside.

Add the onion and garlic to the pan and cook until soft. Stir in the kale. Season with salt and pepper and cook for about 5 minutes, until it collapses and is tender, keep tossing the kale in the pan.

Return the tomatoes to the pan with the sweet potato and stir through to distribute among the kale.

In the meantime, preheat the grill (broiler).

In a bowl, whisk the eggs with the cream, a little grated nutmeg, and season with salt and pepper. Pour over the vegetables and gently swirl the pan to evenly distribute the egg mixture over the vegetables.

Cook on low-medium heat until the frittata is set but still runny on the top.

Place the frying pan under the preheated grill and cook for a few minutes until the frittata is set and golden.

Allow to rest for 3–5 minutes before loosening with a spatula and sliding onto a serving dish.

17½ oz (500 g) sweet potato (kumera)
6–8 stalks of kale
2 tablespoons extra virgin olive oil
9 oz (250 g) grape or cherry tomatoes
1 red onion, thinly sliced
2 garlic cloves, chopped
Salt and freshly ground black pepper
10 extra-large eggs
3 fl oz (90 ml) low-fat cream
Freshly grated nutmeg

Spiced Red Lentils

SERVES 4

This dish is quick and easy to prepare and tastes delicious. Serve this dish with rice, cooked quinoa or just a it is.

8 stalks kale
1 lb 2 oz (500 g) red lentils
6 cups (2½ pints/1.5 litres) water
1 small onion, peeled and halved
1 tablespoon ginger, coarsely grated
2 bay leaves
2 tablespoons olive oil
1 tablespoon ghee butter
4-6 garlic cloves, peeled and sliced
1½ -2 tablespoons cumin seeds
½ -1 teaspoon chilli flakes
Salt
Long fresh chilli, sliced, for garnish
Lemon juice

Thoroughly wash the kale. Remove and discard the tough lower part of the stalk. Finely chop the leaves and the upper, more tender part of the stalk, and set aside.

Pick over the lentils and remove any dirt and grit. Rinse under cold running water, drain and place into a saucepan with the water, onion , ginger and bay leaves. Bring to the boil, reduce the heat, cover and simmer for 15 minutes. Remove any froth/scum that appears on the lentils during cooking.

Remove and discard the onion from the lentils and stir in the kale. Bring back to the boil, reduce the heat and simmer for another 5 minutes.

In the meantime, heat the oil and melt the ghee butter in a small frying pan and when hot, add the garlic and cook until the garlic is golden. Keep an eye on it as garlic tends to burn very quickly.

When the garlic is golden, lift the pan from the heat, add the cumin seeds and chilli flakes, give the pan a good swirl then return to the heat and cook for about 30 seconds, until fragrant.

Season the lentils with salt to taste, pour in the garlic mixture and stir well to combine. Remove the bay leaves.

Serve garnished with sliced fresh chillies, a generous squeeze of lemon juice and a light drizzle of extra virgin olive oil.

Tomato, Mushroom and Chickpea Curry

This is another family favourite that takes very little time to prepare. The flavour keeps on improving with age, can be frozen and is lovely served with cooked quinoa or plain rice.

Thoroughly wash the kale. Remove and discard the thick lower part of the stalk. Chop the leaves and the upper, more tender part of the stalk into small pieces and set aside.

Heat the oil in a large pan, stir in the cinnamon stick and cumin and cook for 1-2 minutes, until fragrant. Stir regularly so that the cumin does not burn.

Add the onion, garlic and chilli and cook 2-3 minutes, until soft. Stir in the turmeric, ground coriander and ground cumin and cook for another 1 minute.

Add the kale to the pan with the tomatoes, season with salt and pepper and cook for 1-2 minutes until the kale wilts.

Pour in the water, cover and simmer on low heat for 8-10 minutes stirring occasionally.

Add the mushrooms and chickpeas and simmer for another 5-8 minutes. Check and adjust the seasoning and also check that the kale is tender.

Remove and discard the cinnamon stick, stir in the coriander leaves and lime juice and serve with a dollop of yogurt.

6 large stalks of kale
2 tablespoons olive oil
1 cinnamon stick
1 tablespoons cumin seeds
1 red onion, finely chopped
3 garlic cloves, finely chopped
1 red or green chilli, chopped
1 tablespoon fresh grated turmeric or 2 teaspoons ground turmeric
2 teaspoons ground coriander
2 teaspoons ground cumin
2 x 14 oz (400 g) cans diced tomatoes
Salt and freshly cracked black pepper
½ cup (4 fl oz/125 ml) water
12½ oz (350 g) button (white) mushrooms, sliced
2 x 14 oz (400 g) cans chickpeas, drained
Salt, to taste
½ cup (bunch) fresh coriander (cilantro), chopped
Juice of 1 lime
Unsweetened Greek (strained plain) yogurt

Vegetable and Coconut Curry

SERVES 6

For a richer sauce, use coconut cream instead of the water. Moist coconut flakes are available at most supermarkets and are lovely to use. However, they can substituted with shredded (dessicated) coconut.

6-8 stalks of kale
2 tablespoons olive oil
1 large brown onion, halved and sliced
4 garlic cloves, finely chopped
1 knob of ginger, peeled and sliced
1 long red or green chilli, sliced
1 tablespoon ground cumin
1 tablespoon ground coriander
1 tablespoon ground turmeric
Small handful curry leaves
17½ oz (500 g) sweet potato (kumera), peeled and diced
1 small eggplant (aubergine), about 1 lb (450 g), diced
2 medium zucchini (courgettes), sliced
2 medium carrots, sliced
½ small cauliflower, cut into florets
Salt and freshly cracked black pepper
14 oz (400 g) can light coconut cream
1 cup (8 fl oz/250 ml) water
Juice of ½ -1 lime
Moist coconut flakes, for garnish

Thoroughly wash the kale. Remove and discard the thick lower part of the stalk. Chop the leaves and the upper, more tender part of the stalk, set aside.

Heat the oil in a large saucepan and cook the onion, garlic, ginger and chilli until soft.

Stir in the cumin, coriander, turmeric and curry leaves and cook until fragrant.

Add the sweet potatoes, eggplant, zucchini, carrots and cauliflower and season with salt and pepper. Stir well to coat with all the spices.

Pour in the coconut cream and the water, bring to the boil, cover and simmer for about 10 minutes, until all the vegetables are almost tender.

Stir in the kale and simmer for another 5 minutes or so, until all the vegetables are tender.

Remove from the heat and stir in as much lime juice as you like before serving garnished with moist coconut flakes. If possible allow the curry to rest for at least half an hour for all the flavours to develop.

Curried Kale with Black Beans

This recipe works well with any type of canned beans such as chickpeas, borlotti beans, turtle beans, etc. You can also add diced potatoes to make this curry stretch further or just add an extra vegetable.

Thoroughly wash the kale, remove and discard the thick lower part of the stalk. Roughly chop the leaves and the more tender upper part of the stalk. Set aside.

Heat the oil in a large pan and sauté the onion, garlic, ginger and chilli for about 2-3 minutes, until soft.

Crack the cardamom pods, remove the seeds and lightly pound in a mortar and pestle.

Add the cardamom seeds and mustard seeds to the pan and cook until the mustard seeds start to pop. Once they pop stir in the curry paste or powder, cumin, coriander, curry leaves, and paprika and cook for another 1 minute or so, stirring regularly so that the spices do not burn.

Add the tomatoes and black beans and water, and bring to the boil, reduce the heat, cover and simmer for 8-10 minutes.

Stir in the kale and simmer covered for another 5 minutes or until the kale is cooked.

Drizzle with lemon or lime juice and serve with a dollop of yogurt.

8-10 large stalks kale
2 tablespoons extra virgin olive oil
1 large red onion, halved, then thinly sliced
3 large garlic cloves, finely chopped
1 tablespoon ginger, freshly grated
1 long red chilli, de-seeded and finely chopped
6-8 green cardamom pods
1 tablespoon mustard seeds
1 tablespoon curry paste or powder
1 teaspoon ground cumin
1 teaspoon ground coriander
Small handful fresh curry leaves
1 teaspoon ground paprika
2 x 14 oz (400 g) cans diced tomatoes
2 x 14 oz (400 g) black beans, drained
1½ cups (12 fl oz/375 ml) water
Salt and freshly ground black pepper
Lemon or lime juice, for serving
Unsweetened Greek (strained plain) yogurt, for garnish

POULTRY

Asian Roast Duck with Stir-Fried Kale

Chicken with Bacon, Kale and Pine Nut Stuffing

Chicken with Mushrooms and Yogurt

Chicken with Leeks and Mustard Sauce

Chicken, Kale and Cashew Stir-Fry

Kumera Boats with Kale and Mustard Chicken

Mushrooms Filled with Turkey and Kale

Spiced Chicken and Almonds with Rice

Asian Roast Duck with Stir-Fried Kale

In this method, the duck is placed in a cold pan, which is then placed over the heat. As the duck cooks, the fat is slowly rendered out of the skin.

Mix all the marinade ingredients together in a large bowl.

Wipe the duck breasts to remove moisture. Using a sharp knife, score the skin into a criss-cross pattern without cutting through to the meat. Place in the bowl with the marinade, coat well and set aside for 20 minutes.

Thoroughly wash the kale. Remove and discard the lower thicker part of the stalk and tear the leaves into pieces. Set aside.

Preheat the oven to 200°C/400°F/Gas mark 6.

Remove the duck from the marinade and pat dry. Place skin-side down, in a cold non-stick ovenproof frying pan. Set over high heat and cook until browned and the skin is crispy. Turn and cook to seal for another 1 minute or so.

Place into the oven, skin-side down, and roast for 10 minutes, or until cooked to your liking, and the skin is crisp. Baste regularly with the marinade during roasting. Allow to rest for 10 minutes before serving.

Meanwhile, heat the vegetable and sesame oil in a large frying pan and sauté the onions, ginger, chilli and garlic until soft. Stir in the kale and cook, tossing continuously until it wilts. Pour in the soy sauce and water and continue cooking for 2-3 minutes, until the kale is tender.

Slice the duck and serve on top of the kale and garnished with extra slices of chilli. Serve with steamed rice.

4 duck breasts, skin on
8-10 large stalks of kale
1-2 tablespoons vegetable oil
1/2 teaspoon sesame oil
1 bunch shallots/spring onions/ scallions, sliced diagonally
1 small knob of ginger, peeled and sliced
1-2 long red chillies, sliced
2 garlic cloves, peeled and finely sliced
2 tablespoons soy sauce
1/2 cup (4 fl oz/125 ml) water

MARINADE
1/2 teaspoon five spice powder
1 teaspoon ground ginger
Pinch of ground cinnamon
1/2 –1 teaspoon dried chilli flakes
1 large garlic clove, finely grated
2 tablespoons light soy sauce
1 teaspoon dark soy sauce
2 tablespoons honey
2 tablespoons Shao-Xing Chinese cooking wine

Note: Shao-Xing cooking wine is available at all Asian grocery stores. Dry sherry can be used as a substitute. Cook the leftover marinade until hot and bubbly for 2-3 minutes to remove any bacteria then pour over duck just before serving.

Chicken with Bacon, Kale and Pine Nut Stuffing

SERVES 4-6

The addition of kale to this stuffing gives it extra texture and bulk with a flavour all its own. A really good way to add kale into a meal.

6 large stalks of kale
1-2 tablespoons extra virgin olive oil, plus extra for drizzling
1 medium onion, finely chopped
2-3 rashers (strips) of bacon, rind discarded, and chopped
2 garlic cloves, finely chopped
1 teaspoon English mustard
1½ cups (3 oz/90 g) fresh breadcrumbs
1 oz (30 g) pine nuts
1 tablespoon fresh thyme leaves
Zest of 1 lemon
Salt and freshly cracked black pepper
1 extra large egg
1 whole chicken, about 4 lb 6 oz-5½ lb (2-2.5 kg)
Lemon juice
Ground sweet paprika

Thoroughly wash the kale. Remove and discard the entire stalk. Finely chop the leaves and set aside.

Preheat the oven to 200°C/400°F/Gas mark 6.

Heat the oil in a large frying pan and sauté the onion and bacon until soft. Add the kale and cook until it wilts, about 3 minutes. Stir in the garlic and take off the heat. Tip into a bowl and leave to cool slightly.

Mix in the mustard, breadcrumbs, pine nuts, thyme and lemon zest. Season. Add the egg then mix to thoroughly combine. The mixture should be moist and hold together.

Remove any excess fat from the chicken, rinse and pat dry with kitchen paper. Neatly tuck the wings at the back of the chicken.

Place the stuffing into the cavity and secure the opening with a small metal skewer. Put in a baking dish and drizzle with some extra virgin olive oil and a generous squeeze of lemon juice. Season the chicken with a little salt and pepper and sprinkle with ground paprika.

Bake for 30 minutes until golden all over. Remove from the oven and cover with non-stick baking or parchment paper followed by a sheet of foil.

Reduce the oven temperature to 180°C/350°F/Gas mark 4. Return to the oven and bake for another 1 hour, or until the chicken is cooked. Baste every now and then with pan juices. The chicken is cooked when the juices run clear when a metal skewer is inserted into the thickest part of the thigh area. Cover with foil and allow to rest for 15-20 minutes before serving.

Chicken with Mushrooms and Yogurt

SERVES 4

This is a one-pot meal that's great for mid-week cooking – only one to wash up afterwards! Veal can be substituted for the chicken.

6-8 large stalks of kale

2-3 tablespoons extra virgin olive oil

1 lb 10 oz (750 g) chicken breasts cut into bite-size pieces

1 teaspoon ground sweet paprika

6 shallots/spring onions/scallions, sliced

1 lb (450 g) button (white) mushrooms, sliced

3 garlic cloves, finely chopped

1 cup (8 fl oz/250 ml) chicken stock

Salt and freshly cracked black pepper

½ teaspoon grated nutmeg

3-4 tablespoons Greek (strained plain) yogurt

Lemon juice

Thoroughly wash the kale. Remove and discard the thick lower part of the stalk. Chop the leaves and the upper, more tender part of the stalk and then set aside.

Heat the oil in a large pan, coat the chicken with the paprika, add to the pan and brown all over until almost cooked. Remove from the pan and set aside.

Add the shallots, mushrooms and garlic and cook until soft and the mushrooms reduce.

Pour in the stock and stir in the kale. Season with salt and pepper and add the nutmeg. Cover and simmer on low heat about 5 minutes.

Return the chicken to the pan and continue cooking for another 5 minutes until the kale is tender and the chicken is cooked through.

Stir in the yogurt. Check and adjust the seasoning and simmer over low heat for another 2-3 minutes, until the sauce starts to bubble.

Add the lemon juice, to taste, over the chicken and serve with plain rice or cooked quinoa.

Chicken with Leeks and Mustard Sauce

I love the creamy mustard sauce in this recipe. The kale absorbs the flavours of the sauce really well. I usually serve this dish with either cooked quinoa, rice or boiled/steamed baby new potatoes.

Thoroughly wash the kale. Remove and discard the thick lower part of the stalk. Chop the leaves and the upper more tender part of the stalk into pieces and set aside.

Mix the flour and paprika together and lightly coat the chicken in this mixture.

Heat the oil in a large, deep frying pan until hot, add the chicken and brown on both sides.

Remove the chicken from the pan, cover and keep warm.

Add the leeks to the pan and sauté until lightly golden and tender. Stir in the garlic and cook for another 1 minute.

Stir in the mustard, then pour in the wine and cook on high heat for 1-2 minutes, until the alcohol has evaporated. Make sure you scrape the base of the pan to release all the flavours that have stuck to the base.

Pour in the stock, then add the thyme leaves and kale. When the kale has softened a little and collapsed, return the chicken to the pan and season with salt and pepper.

Bring to the boil, reduce the heat, cover and simmer for about 10-12 minutes, until the chicken and kale are cooked and the sauce has thickened. If the sauce is too runny, cook uncovered on high heat for another 2 minutes or so until the sauce has thickened.

Serve on polenta, rice or mashed potatoes.

8-10 stalks of kale

½ cup (2 oz/60 g) flour

½ teaspoon ground paprika

4 chicken half-breast fillets, skinned, trimmed and left whole

2 tablespoons extra virgin olive oil

2 leeks, trimmed, washed and sliced

2 garlic cloves, chopped

2 tablespoons Dijon mustard

¾ cup (6 fl oz/175 ml) white wine

2 cups (16 fl oz/500 ml) chicken stock

A few sprigs of fresh thyme

Salt and freshly ground pepper

Lemon juice

Chicken, Kale and Cashew Stir-Fry

Shao-Xing wine is an Asian cooking wine and is available at most Asian grocery stores. Dry sherry is a good substitute.

Place the chicken into a bowl with the garlic and kecap manis. Mix well and leave to marinate while you prepare the other ingredients.

Thoroughly wash the kale. Remove and discard the lower thick part of the stalk and tear the leaves into pieces.

Heat a little of the oils in a wok or large deep-sided frying pan until hot, add the cashews and toss until they are lightly golden. Transfer from the pan onto some kitchen paper and set aside.

Add the remaining oils to the pan, heat until hot and cook the chicken in two batches over high heat for 3–4 minutes, until golden and cooked, remove from the pan and set aside.

Add a little more oil to the wok, if necessary, then add the chilli, ginger, capsicum and beans, and stir-fry for about 2–3 minutes, or until tender but still crisp.

Add the shallots and kale and stir-fry for 2–3 minutes until the kale wilts.

Mix together the soy sauce, dry sherry or wine, water and the cornflour in a small bowl, then add to the vegetables and cook for 1 minute.

Return the chicken and cashews to the pan and stir until well combined and the chicken has heated through.

Serve with steamed rice or with some noodles stirred through.

1 lb 10 oz (750 g) chicken breast fillets, trimmed and sliced into thin strips
2 garlic cloves, finely chopped
1 tablespoon kecap manis
1 bunch of kale, about 10 stalks
3 oz (90 g) raw unsalted cashews
2 tablespoons oil
1/2 teaspoon sesame oil
1 long red chilli, sliced
1 small knob of ginger, finely chopped
1 red capsicum (bell pepper), diced
4 1/2 oz (125 g) green beans, de-stringed and halved
6 shallots/spring onions/ scallions, thickly sliced diagonally
2 tablespoons soy sauce
2 tablespoons dry sherry or Shao-Xing wine
1/2 cup (4 fl oz/125 ml) water
1 generous teaspoon cornflour (corn starch)

Kumera Boats with Kale and Mustard Chicken

SERVES 2-4

Choose well rounded and even-sized sweet potatoes for this dish so that they will sit well balanced on the baking sheet.

2 evenly shaped sweet
   potatoes (kumera)
   about 1 lb 10 oz (750 g)
   each
8 stalks of kale
1-2 tablespoons extra virgin
   olive oil
4-6 shallots/spring onions/
   scallions, sliced
1 garlic clove, finely
   chopped
1 lb (450 g) minced
   (ground) chicken
1 teaspoon fresh rosemary
   leaves, chopped
Zest of ½ lemon
2 teaspoons English
   mustard
Juice of ½ lemon
Salt and freshly cracked
   black pepper
¾ cup (3 oz/90 g)
   Cheddar (tasty) cheese,
   grated

Preheat the oven to 190°C/375°F/Gas mark 5 and line a baking sheet with non-stick baking or parchment paper.

Place the whole unpeeled sweet potatoes onto the baking sheet and bake for about 45 minutes to 1 hour, or until tender. Remove from the oven and leave to cool slightly. Reduce the oven temperature to 180°C/350°F/Gas mark 4.

In the meantime, thoroughly wash the kale, remove and discard the entire stalk and finely chop the leaves. Set aside.

Heat the oil in a frying pan and sauté the shallots and garlic for 1-2 minutes.

Stir in the minced chicken and continue cooking until the chicken is no longer pink, then stir in the rosemary and lemon zest.

Add the finely chopped kale and continue cooking for 3-4 minutes until the kale has collapsed.

Stir in the mustard, lemon juice and season with salt and pepper to taste.

Cut the potato in half lengthways and remove some of the centre, leaving a thickish shell. Try not to remove too much of the centre as shells are not as strong as those of ordinary potatoes.

Combine the potato pulp with the kale and chicken and fold in the cheese.

Pile the chicken mixture into the potato cases, then return to the oven and bake for 10-15 minutes, or until the chicken is fully cooked and the cheese has melted.

Mushrooms Filled with Turkey and Kale

A particularly lovely dish to serve as a light lunch. Easy to prepare, satisfying and delicious. A salad and a glass of wine are all you need to serve with it.

Preheat the oven to 180°C/350°F/Gas mark 4. Line a baking sheet with non-stick baking or parchment paper.

Thoroughly wash the kale. Remove and discard the thick lower part of the stalks and finely chop the leaves and some of the more tender, upper stalks.

Gently wipe over the mushrooms and remove the stalk.

Heat the oil in a large non-stick frying pan and sauté the turkey mince until sealed all over and starting to take on some colour.

Add the bacon and onion and cook for 3-4 minutes.

Stir in the tomato paste, garlic and thyme and cook for about 1 minute.

Add the kale to the pan and cook until it starts to wilt.

Pour in the stock or water, season with a little salt and a generous grind of pepper and cook, covered, for about 5 minutes, until the kale is tender.

Do not allow the kale to dry out, if it looks like it will dry, add a little more water to the pan. Remove the pan from the heat.

Divide the mixture into six and fill the underside of each mushroom with the filling. Mix the cheeses together and scatter over each mushroom.

Place the mushrooms on the prepared baking sheet, drizzle a little olive oil over each one and bake for about 15-20 minutes.

Serve with sprigs of thyme and a salad.

6-8 large stalks of kale

6 extra-large flat mushrooms

1-2 tablespoons extra virgin olive oil, plus extra for drizzling

17½ oz (500 g) minced turkey

2 rashers (strips) bacon, rind removed and chopped

1 medium red onion, finely chopped

1 tablespoon tomato paste or purée

2 garlic cloves, finely chopped

1 tablespoon fresh thyme leaves, plus extra for serving

1 cup (8 fl oz/250 ml) chicken stock or water

Salt and freshly cracked black pepper

Cheddar (tasty) cheese, grated

Parmesan, grated

Spiced Chicken and Almonds with Rice

SERVES 4-6

Apart from being delicious this dish is all prepared in one pot. Place it in the centre of the table and let everyone help themselves.

8 stalks of kale

1½ cups (10½ oz/300 g) basmati rice

2-3 tablespoons extra virgin olive oil

1 large onion, halved and sliced

6-7 green cardamom pods

2-3 long red chillies, left whole

3-4 garlic cloves, peeled and sliced

1 thumb size piece of fresh ginger, peeled and finely sliced

1 cinnamon stick

2 teaspoons ground coriander

2 teaspoons ground cumin

1 tablespoon fresh turmeric, grated

750g (1 lb 10 oz) chicken breast fillets, skinned

1 cup (5 oz/150 g) sultanas (golden raisins)

3 cups (24 fl oz/750 ml) water or chicken stock

Salt and freshly ground black pepper

4½ oz (125 g) whole blanched almonds, toasted

Lemon juice

Thoroughly wash the kale. Remove and discard the thick lower part of the stalk. Finely chop the leaves and the upper, more tender parts of the stalk and set aside.

Cover the rice with boiling water and leave to stand while you prepare the other ingredients.

Heat the oil in a large deep frying pan on medium heat until hot. Add the onions and cook until they are soft and just start to change colour.

In the meantime, crush the cardamom pods in a mortar and pestle. Discard the pods and crush the seeds until fine.

Add the cardamom, chillies, garlic, ginger, cinnamon stick, coriander, cumin and fresh turmeric to the pan and continue cooking for 1-2 minutes, until fragrant. Stir regularly so that the onions and garlic don't burn.

Cut the chicken into thin strips, add to the pan and stir well. Continue cooking until the chicken is almost cooked through.

Drain the rice and add to the pan with the sultanas and water or stock, season with salt to taste, bring to the boil, reduce the heat, cover and simmer for about 5 minutes.

Stir in the kale, cover and continue to simmer for another 5-7 minutes, until the rice is cooked and the water is absorbed.

Sprinkle the almonds over the top and serve with a good squeeze of lemon juice.

MEAT

Baked Veal and Pork Rolls with Tomato Sauce

Beef Stir-Fry with Snow Peas and Kale

Italian Pizza Loaf

Kale Lasagne

Beef in Red Sauce with Kale Polenta

Mexican Beef

Penne with Italian Sausage

Shepherd's Pie

Baked Veal and Pork Rolls with Tomato Sauce

SERVES 6

Cavolo nero (Tuscan kale) works best in this recipe as the leaves are flat and, once blanched, are quite pliable. Leaves should be totally immersed in the water when blanching. You will need to choose large kale leaves for this recipe so that the filling can be totally wrapped inside the leaves. The amount of rolls made will depend on the size of the kale leaves.

20-24 large stalks cavolo nero (Tuscan kale)
2-3 tablespoons extra virgin olive oil
1 large onion, very finely chopped
2 garlic cloves, finely grated
9 oz (250 g) minced (ground) veal
9 oz (250 g) minced (ground) pork
14 oz (400 g) can diced tomatoes
Salt and freshly cracked black pepper
1½ cups (10½ oz/300 g) cooked rice
½ cup (bunch) finely chopped parsley, plus extra to garnish
2 eggs, lightly beaten
2-3 tablespoons Parmesan, grated, plus extra to serve

Thoroughly wash the kale, fold each stalk in half lengthways and trim off the thicker lower part of the stalk with a knife. You should be left with a whole leaf that has a split in the lower end.

Bring a large pan of salted water to the boil and blanche the leaves for about 5-7 minutes. Drain and refresh under cold running water to stop the cooking process. Drain again and set aside.

To make the meat filling, heat the oil in a large frying pan and sauté the onion until golden. Stir in the garlic and cook until fragrant. Add the veal and pork mince and continue cooking until browned, breaking up any lumps in the meat as you go. Add the tomatoes, season with salt and pepper and cook, uncovered, on low-medium heat for about 10 minutes. Remove from the heat and leave to cool.

When cooled to just warm, stir in the rice, parsley, eggs and Parmesan.

Preheat the oven to 180°C/350°F/Gas mark 4.

Arrange each kale leaf on a flat surface and bring the split halves together. Place some of the mince mixture on the split half end and roll tightly tucking in the sides as you go. Place the rolls side by side in a single layer in a large baking dish.

To make the tomato sauce, heat the oil on a deep frying pan and sauté the onion until golden. Stir in the garlic, tomato paste and sugar, and cook for 1 -2 minutes. Add the passata and water, season with salt and pepper, cover and simmer for 10-15 minutes until the sauce starts to thicken.

Pour the tomato sauce over the top and bake for about 30 minutes.

Serve garnished with extra Parmesan and chopped parsley.

TOMATO SAUCE

2 tablespoons extra virgin olive oil

1 medium onion, finely chopped

2 garlic cloves, finely chopped

3 tablespoons tomato paste

½ -1 teaspoon sugar

14 oz (400 g) passata

1½ cups (12 fl oz/375 ml) water

Beef Stir-Fry with Snow Peas and Kale

SERVES 4

This is a very quick-and-easy dish to prepare especially after a long day at work. The use of kale instead of the usual Asian greens add texture, bulk and a delicious taste.

6-8 stalks cavolo nero (Tuscan kale)

1½ cups (12 fl oz/375 ml) beef stock

1 generous tablespoon cornflour (corn starch)

3 tablespoons tamari soy sauce

1 teaspoon brown sugar

2 tablespoons olive oil

1 teaspoon sesame oil

1 lb 6 oz (600 g) rump steak, cut into thin strips

4½ oz (125 g) snow peas (mange tout), string removed

1 knob of ginger (about 1½ in (4 cm), sliced

3 garlic cloves, peeled and sliced

1 long red chilli, sliced

4 shallots/spring onions/ scallions, sliced

Thoroughly wash the kale. Remove and discard the thick lower part of the stalk. Roughly chop the leaves and the upper, more tender part of the stalk and set aside.

Mix together the stock, flour, soy sauce and sugar. Stir until the flour and sugar have dissolved. Set aside.

Heat the olive and sesame oils in a wok or a large, deep frying pan set over high heat until very hot. Add the steak and stir-fry in batches for about 3-4 minutes, or until browned and cooked. Transfer each batch from the pan, set aside and keep warm.

Add a little more oil to the wok, if necessary, heat on high heat until hot and then add the kale and the snow peas, ginger, garlic and chilli, and toss for about 1-2 minutes, until fragrant and the kale has started to wilt.

Stir the stock mixture, then pour into the wok and simmer for 3-5 minutes, until the kale is tender and the sauce has thickened. Stir the wok regularly during cooking.

Return the meat to the wok, stir through the shallots and toss until heated through, about 2-3 minutes.

Serve with rice.

Note: I find that cavolo nero (Tuscan kale), works best in this recipe. Sometimes you can find bunches of cavolo nero that also have lots of very small, young and tender leaves. These can be left whole and there is no need to remove any of the stalks.

Italian Pizza Loaf

The quantity of ingredients required for this recipe may vary depending on the size of the bread loaf.

Mix the olive oil, vinegar and oregano together in a bowl and set aside.

Thoroughly wash the kale. Remove and discard the lower tough stalks and finely slice the leaves and the upper, more tender parts of the stalk.

Heat the olive oil in a large frying pan, add the kale and cook for 5-7 minutes, until it has wilted and is tender. Stir in the garlic and cook until fragrant. Remove from the heat, season with salt and pepper and set aside.

Slice a lid off the top of the bread, remove most of the inside dough and drizzle the inside with a little of the olive oil and vinegar mixture.

Place the cheese in a layer inside the bread. Top with half of the kale mixture, then the capsicums.

Layer the olives on top followed by the salami, tomatoes, and onion, and season well. Scatter the remaining kale on top and drizzle with remaining dressing.

Top with the mozzarella and add the Parmesan.

Replace the bread lid and tightly wrap in a sheet of non-stick baking or parchment paper followed by a sheet of foil. Leave to stand with a weight on top for about 20-30 minutes, longer if possible.

Preheat the oven to 190°C/375°F/Gas mark 5. Remove the weight and place the wrapped bread on a baking sheet and bake for 30-40 minutes, until the bread is crunchy and all the filling is hot.

Remove from the oven and leave to rest for 10 minutes before slicing and serving.

3 tablespoons extra virgin olive oil

1 tablespoons balsamic vinegar

1 teaspoons dried oregano leaves

About 10 stalks cavolo nero (Tuscan kale)

1 tablespoon extra virgin olive oil

2 garlic cloves, finely chopped

1 Italian style *pane di casa* loaf of bread

5 oz (150 g) Cheddar (tasty) cheese, sliced

4½ oz (125 g) char-grilled capsicums (bell peppers), drained

18 Kalamata olives, pits removed and flesh halved

4½ oz (125 g) salami, thinly sliced, (optional)

2 ripe but firm tomatoes, sliced

1 Spanish (Bermuda) onion, thinly sliced

Salt and freshly cracked black pepper

5 oz (150 g) mozzarella cheese, sliced

1 tablespoon Parmesan shavings

Kale Lasagne

SERVES 6

This recipe is made using homemade pasta dough, which is made with kale. The pasta is layered with sautéed kale and meat sauce, and then baked with a herby low-fat cheese topping. It freezes beautifully and is really worth making.

12 large stalks of cavolo nero (Tuscan kale)

2 tablespoons extra virgin olive oil

1 large onion, finely chopped

1 lb 10 oz (750 g) minced (ground) beef

3 garlic cloves, finely chopped

2 tablespoons tomato paste

2 teaspoons dried oregano

24 fl oz (700 ml) passata

2½ cups (generous 1 pint/ 625 ml) water

Salt and freshly cracked black pepper

1 quantity fresh pasta dough, see page 83

Thoroughly wash the kale. Remove and discard most of the thick stalk. Place the leaves into a heatproof bowl and cover with boiling water. Let stand for 5 minutes, then drain and set aside.

Heat the oil in a large pan and sauté the onion on high heat until golden. Add the minced beef and continue cooking until browned all over. Break up any lumps as you go.

Stir in the garlic and cook for 1 minute, then add the tomato paste and oregano and cook for another 1–2 minutes.

Pour in the passata and water and season with salt and pepper to taste. Bring to the boil, reduce the heat and simmer on low heat, covered, for 25–30 minutes.

Make the kale lasagne sheets. Roll thin.

Preheat the oven to 200°C/400°F/Gas mark 6. Line a baking sheet with non-stick baking or parchment paper.

To make the cheese topping, mix all the ingredients together in a bowl.

Spread a thin layer of meat sauce over the base of a 13 x 9 x 2½ in (33 x 23 x 6½ cm) lasagne dish. Top with a layer of lasagne sheets, then spread one-third of the meat sauce on top. Cover the meat sauce with four of the blanched kale leaves and a scatter of the cheese topping. (continued overleaf)

Kale Lasagne (cont'd)

CHEESE TOPPING

17½ oz (500 g) low-fat cottage cheese (farmers' cheese)

13 oz (375 g) low-fat ricotta cheese

1 cup (250 ml/8 fl oz) low-fat (semi-skimmed) milk

3 tablespoons Parmesan, grated, plus extra for garnishing

1-2 tablespoons fresh oregano leaves, chopped

Salt and freshly cracked black pepper

Repeat this process twice more, finishing with a layer of lasagne sheet.

Cover with the remaining cheese topping and sprinkle some extra grated Parmesan on top.

Place the lasagne dish onto the baking sheet (the sheet will collect any overflow from the lasagne as it is cooking and cut down on the washing up) and bake for 25-35 minutes, until bubbly and golden on top. Let stand for 20-30 minutes before cutting.

Note: You will not need the whole quantity of pasta dough. Any leftover dough can be frozen.

You could also add finely chopped kale leaves (no stalks) into the sauce while it is cooking

Beef in Red Sauce with Kale Polenta

SERVES 4

The beef in red sauce could be prepared ahead and frozen. The kale can also be prepared and cooked in advance so that all you need to do before serving is prepare the polenta. Stir the pre-cooked kale through the polenta and heat the beef.

Heat the oil in a pan set over high heat. Add the beef and brown all over. Add the onion and garlic. Sauté until soft. Stir in the tomato paste and cook for 1 minute.

Add the tomatoes, oregano and water and season well. Bring to the boil, reduce the heat, cover and simmer for 45–60 minutes, or until tender.

To make the kale polenta, thoroughly wash the kale. Remove and discard the entire thick part of the stalk and finely chop the leaves.

Heat the oil in large frying pan and sauté the shallots and garlic until soft. Stir in the kale and cook for 4–5 minutes, until the kale has wilted and is cooked. Keep stirring and tossing the kale regularly during cooking. Set aside.

For the polenta, pour the water into a pan set over high heat and bring to the boil. Slowly add the polenta in a fine, steady stream stirring constantly with a metal whisk until the polenta is fully incorporated. Lower the heat and continue cooking, stirring constantly until the polenta is soft, thick and creamy and you cannot feel any fine grains.

Stir in the Parmesan, butter, and salt and pepper, then stir in the kale and just leave on the heat long enough for the kale to be heated through.

Serve garnished with shavings of Parmesan.

2 tablespoons extra virgin olive oil
750 g (1 lb 10 oz) chuck fillet steak, cubed
1 large onion, finely chopped
2–3 garlic cloves, finely chopped
1 tablespoon tomato paste
14 oz (400 g) can diced tomatoes
1 teaspoon dried oregano
2 cups (16 fl oz/500 ml) hot water
Salt and freshly cracked black pepper

KALE POLENTA
6 stalks cavolo nero (Tuscan kale)
2 tablespoons extra virgin olive oil
4 shallots/spring onions/scallions, sliced
1 garlic clove
5½ cups (2¼ pints/1.3 litres) hot chicken or vegetable stock or water
1½ cups (9 oz/250 g) fine polenta
4 tablespoons Parmesan, grated, plus extra shavings, for garnish
2 tablespoons butter

Mexican Beef

SERVES 4-6

A really good dish to make and serve with rice. It is quick and easy to prepare and an ideal dish to make if you are cooking meals in advance to serve through the week. The flavour just keeps on improving.

1 bunch cavolo nero (Tuscan kale)

2 tablespoons extra virgin olive oil

1 onion, halved and finely sliced

1 lb 10 oz (750 g) minced (ground) beef

3 garlic cloves, finely chopped

2 teaspoons cumin

2 teaspoons sweet paprika

1 teaspoon dried oregano

1-2 long red chillies, sliced

1-2 tablespoons tomato paste

1½ cups (12 fl oz/375 ml) water

2 cups (12 oz/350 g) frozen corn

Rice, to serve

Slices of fresh avocado

Lime juice, to serve

Sour cream, to serve

Fresh coriander (cilantro) leaves, for garnish

Thoroughly wash the kale. Remove and discard the thick lower part of the stalk. Chop the leaves and upper, more tender part of the stalk and set aside.

Heat the oil in a large, deep frying pan and cook the onion until soft and golden.

Add the minced beef and continue cooking until browned. Stir in the garlic and cook for about 30 seconds.

Stir in the cumin, paprika, oregano, chillies and tomato paste, and cook for 1 minute.

Pour in the water and season with salt. Cover and cook on low heat for about 5 minutes.

Add the kale and the corn. Stir well and cook for another 5 minutes, until the kale wilts and is cooked.

Serve over rice with slices of avocado that have had lime juice sprinkled over them and with a dollop sour cream and finely chopped coriander leaves.

Penne with Italian Sausage

The kale really complements the spices used in the sausages and the pasta just rounds it all up. Make sure you use lots of Parmesan grated over the top.

Thoroughly wash the kale, remove and discard the lower thick part of the stalk and chop the leaves into strips. Set aside.

Remove the skin from the sausages and squeeze the meat out of the sausage skins and form into small balls. Set aside.

Bring a large pan of salted water to a rolling boil and cook the pasta until just before it gets to the *al dente* stage.

While the pasta is cooking, heat the oil in a large, deep frying pan and cook the meat balls until browned and cooked through, remove from the pan.

Add the onion, garlic and chilli flakes to the pan and cook until soft. Stir in the kale and white wine and continue cooking until the wine has evaporated and the kale has wilted.

Cover and cook on a gentle heat until the kale is tender, about 5 minutes. Return the meat balls to the pan.

Drain the pasta but keep about 1 cup (8 fl oz/250 ml) of the water it was cooked in.

Add the pasta to the meat balls and kale, mix well and season with salt and pepper.

Cook for about 3-5 minutes to finish cooking the pasta and to allow all the ingredients and flavours to combine. Add a little of the reserved pasta water if the pan seems too dry.

Serve with Parmesan and a little more cracked black pepper.

6-8 stalks cavalo nero (Tuscan) kale
1 lb 10 oz (750 g) Italian sausages
13 oz (375 g) penne
2 tablespoons extra virgin olive oil
1 large red onion, chopped
3-4 garlic cloves, sliced
½ -1 teaspoon dried chilli flakes
2/3 cup (5½ fl oz/160 ml) white wine
Salt and freshly cracked black pepper
Parmesan, grated, for garnish

Shepherd's Pie

SERVES 4

An old family favourite. The addition of kale to the traditional lamb base adds texture, bulk and a very healthy green vegetable.

2¼ lb (1 kg) potatoes, peeled and cut into chunks
6-8 large stalks of kale
1-2 tablespoons extra virgin olive oil
1 large onion, finely chopped
2 medium carrots, finely diced
1 lb 2 oz (500 g) minced (ground) lamb
2 garlic cloves, chopped
1 tablespoon tomato paste
1 tablespoon Worcestershire sauce
3 cups (24 fl oz/750 ml) water or beef stock
Salt and freshly cracked black pepper
1 cup (4 oz/115 g) frozen peas
Pinch of nutmeg
½ cup (4 fl oz/125 ml) milk
Ground paprika

Cook the potatoes in salted boiling water until tender.

While the potatoes are cooking, wash the kale thoroughly. Discard the tough lower stalks, then finely chop the leaves and the upper, more tender parts of the stalk. Set aside.

Heat the oil in a large frying pan and sauté the onion on high heat until soft and golden, stir in the diced carrot and cook for 2-3 minutes. Add the lamb and continue cooking on high heat until browned all over, breaking up any lumps in the meat as you go.

Stir in the garlic and cook for about 1 minute until fragrant. Add the tomato paste and cook for another 1 minute.

Stir in the Worcestershire sauce and water or stock and season with salt and pepper. Bring to the boil, reduce the heat, cover and simmer on low heat for 5 minutes.

Add the kale in batches and stir until it wilts. Stir in the peas then taste and adjust the seasoning. Cover and simmer for about 3-5 minutes.

In the meantime preheat the oven to 200°/400°F/Gas mark 6.

When the potatoes are cooked, drain well and mash with the milk until smooth. Season with salt and pepper to taste and stir in the nutmeg.

Place the lamb mixture into an ovenproof dish and spread the potato mixture on top.

Dust with ground paprika and bake for 20-30 minutes, until the mashed potato is golden.

SEAFOOD

Curried Shrimp with Toasted Coconut Quinoa

Baked Salmon Fillets with Kale Pesto

Fish and Shrimp Pie

Shrimp and Kale Risotto

Salmon Fishcakes with Sweet Chilli Yogurt

Tuna and Kale Mornay

Curried Shrimp with Toasted Coconut Quinoa

One of my favourite ways to have shrimp is in a curry sauce. The combination of the kale with the curry and the shrimps adds a lovely richness and an unusual combination that is full of flavour. Goes really well with the quinoa cooked in coconut.

Thoroughly wash the kale. Remove and discard the thick lower part of the stalk. Chop the leaves and the upper, more tender part of the stalk and set aside.

Heat the oil in a large pan and sauté the onion on medium heat until soft and golden. Add the garlic and chilli and cook for a few seconds until soft.

Stir in the curry powder, turmeric and garam masala and cook for about 1 minute until fragrant. Keep an eye on the spices so they don't burn.

Pour in the soy sauce and water or stock and scrape the base of the pan to release all the flavours that have developed.

Stir in the kale, season with salt and pepper, bring to the boil, reduce the heat, cover and simmer for about 5 minutes.

Add the shrimp to the kale, bring back to the boil, reduce the heat, cover and simmer on low heat for another 7–10 minutes, until the shrimp are cooked.

6 large stalks kale
2 tablespoons olive oil
2 medium onions, halved then sliced
3 garlic cloves, finely chopped
1 green or red chilli, sliced
2 teaspoons curry powder
1 tablespoon freshly grated turmeric or 1 teaspoon ground dried turmeric
½ teaspoon ground garam masala
2 tablespoons soy sauce
2 cups (16 fl oz/500 ml) water or fish stock
Salt and freshly cracked black pepper
1 kg (2¼ lb) green shrimp, peeled and deveined, tails intact
1 tablespoon cornflour (corn starch)
Juice 1 lemon

Curried Shrimp with Toasted Coconut Quinoa (cont'd)

TOASTED COCONUT QUINOA

2 cups (12 oz/350 g) quinoa, rinsed

2½ cups (generous 1 pint/625 ml) water

14 oz (400 g) can coconut milk

1 cup (3 oz/90 g) unsweetened shredded (dessicated) coconut flakes

Lemon juice

Mix the cornflour with a little cold water to form a paste.

Slowly drizzle the cornflour mixture into the shrimp mixture stirring constantly until the sauce thickens.

Check and adjust the seasoning and add as much of the lemon juice as you like.

Meanwhile, to make the toasted coconut quinoa, place the quinoa in a medium pan with the water and coconut milk. Bring to the boil, then reduce the heat, cover and simmer for 12–15 minutes, until all the liquid is absorbed.

Dry roast the coconut flakes in a small non-stick frying pan, turning and tossing regularly so that they don't burn and are a light golden colour. Mix through the quinoa and arrange on a serving plate. Top with the curried shrimp mixture.

Baked Salmon Fillets with Kale Pesto

This is a great dish for a dinner party when you want to serve something different but very special. It is full of flavour and very easy to prepare. It can be made in advance and cooked just before serving. A really good way to introduce someone to kale if they have never tasted it before. Lovely served with steamed/boiled baby new potatoes and green beans.

Preheat the oven to 180°C/350°F/Gas mark 4. Line a baking dish with non-stick baking or parchment paper.

Prepare the fish, season with a little salt and pepper and placing skin side down in the baking dish.

Place a generous amount of kale pesto on top of each fish fillet, covering it completely, and bake for 15-20 minutes ,or until the salmon is cooked to your preference.

Remove the fish from the oven, cover loosely with foil to keep warm and allow to rest for about 5 minutes.

Squeeze lemon juice on top of each piece of salmon and serve garnished with thin slices of lemon and with some grated Parmesan scattered on top.

4 salmon fillets, each about 7 oz (200 g)
Salt and freshly cracked black peeper
1 quantity Kale Pesto (see page 84)
Lemon juice
Lemon slices, for garnish
Parmesan, grated, for garnish

Note: If you have some pesto leftover, you can use it with pasta or over rice or cooked quinoa. Replace the salmon with chicken breast fillets in this recipe, if you like.

Fish and Shrimp Pie

SERVES 6-8

You can use whatever combination of fish you like. If you don't like smoked fish, substitute the amount specified with another type of fish.

2¼ lb (1 kg) potatoes, peeled and cubed

6 stalks kale

12 oz (350 g) skinless white fish fillets

12 oz (350 g) skinless salmon fillet

12 oz (350 g) smoked haddock or cod

1 onion, peeled and halved and 1 small onion, finely chopped

4 cloves

2 bay leaves

3 cups (24 fl oz/750 ml) milk

1 lb (450 g) cooked peeled shrimp

2-3 tablespoons lemon juice

3½ tablespoons butter

1 small onion, finely chopped

3 tablespoons flour

3 hard-boiled eggs

Boil the potatoes in a large pan of salted water until tender.

Thoroughly wash the kale and remove most of the thick stalk. Chop the leaves into small pieces and set aside.

Remove and discard any bones from the fish and place the fish into a large deep frying pan. Stud the two onion halves with the cloves, and add to the pan with the bay leaves and the milk.

Bring the milk to the boil, then immediately reduce the heat, cover and simmer for about 8-10 minutes.

Transfer the fish into a bowl using a slotted spoon.

Add the kale to the milk in the pan. Simmer for about 5 minutes until the kale wilts and is tender. Drain the kale and reserve the milk. Discard the clove-studded onion and bay leaves.

Flake the fish into pieces and make sure all the bones have been removed. Add the kale to the fish with the shrimp and lemon juice, and season with salt and pepper then gently mix together.

Melt 1½ tablespoons of the butter in a saucepan, add the finely chopped onion and cook until the onion is soft and just starts to turn golden. Stir in the flour to form a roux, then slowly pour in the reserved milk (there should be about 2 cups/16 fl oz/500 ml of reserved milk) and stir constantly, until the sauce starts to bubble and thicken. Remove from the heat.

Pour the sauce over the fish, shrimp and kale and gently mix to combine. Tip into a baking dish.

Cut the eggs into quarters and arrange over the fish.

Preheat the oven to 200°C/400°F/Gas mark 6. Line a baking sheet with non-stick baking or parchment paper.

Drain the potatoes well and using a fork, mash with the remaining butter until smooth. Spread over the top of the fish and lightly fluff with a fork.

Place the baking dish onto the prepared baking sheet and bake for 35–45 minutes, until golden.

Shrimp and Kale Risotto

SERVES 4

Italians usually never, ever sprinkle Parmesan on any seafood pasta or risotto dish. In my family we have always done so and my dear Italian grandmother would be horrified if she thought we were doing it any differently now. I will, however, leave it up to you to decide.

8-10 large stalks cavolo nero (Tuscan kale)
2-3 tablespoons extra virgin olive oil
1 onion, finely chopped
3 shallots/scallions/spring onions, sliced
2 large garlic cloves, finely chopped
12 oz (350 g) arborio rice
½ cup (4 fl oz/125 ml) white wine
Salt and freshly cracked black pepper
5-6 cups (2-2¼ pints/1.3-1.5 litres) hot seafood or chicken stock
1 lb 10 oz (750 g) peeled and deveined green shrimp
Knob of butter
Parmesan, grated (optional)
Lemon juice

Thoroughly wash the kale. Remove and discard the thick lower part of the stalk and finely chop the leaves. Set aside.

Heat the oil in a large saucepan and cook the onions and shallots over medium heat until soft. Stir in the garlic and cook for another 30 seconds or so, until fragrant.

Stir in the rice and cook until the colour changes to opaque. Pour in the wine, stir and cook until the alcohol has evaporated and all the liquid has been absorbed. Season the rice with a little salt and a generous grind of pepper.

In another pan, heat the stock until hot and leave on a low simmer on the stove throughout the cooking time.

Add the stock to the rice one ladleful at a time and stir continuously until each ladleful is absorbed before adding the next.

After about 15-20 minutes, add the shrimp and continue stirring and adding the stock for another 5 minutes.

Stir in the kale and continue cooking for another 3-5 minutes, until the rice is fully cooked and the kale has wilted.

Stir in the butter, taste and adjust the seasoning if necessary. The rice should be soft and creamy.

Stir in the Parmesan, if using, drizzle with lemon juice and serve immediately.

Salmon Fishcakes with Sweet Chilli Yogurt

This recipe makes eight good sized portions, depending on appetites and the accompaniments served with them. Serve one or two fishcakes per person.

Preheat the oven to 200°C/400°F/Gas mark 6. Line a large baking sheet with non-stick baking or parchment paper.

Remove any bones from the salmon and place on the prepared sheet. Season with salt and pepper and drizzle with a little extra virgin olive oil.

Bake for about 12–15 minutes, or until cooked. Remove from the oven and set aside. Leave the oven on and line another baking sheet with non-stick baking or parchment paper.

In the meantime, cook the potatoes in salted boiling water until tender.

Thoroughly wash the kale. Remove and discard most of the thick lower part of the stalk and finely chop the leaves.

Heat the oil in a large frying pan and sauté the shallots until soft and golden. Add the kale and cook for about 3–5 minutes, until it wilts and is tender. Keep tossing the kale while it is cooking. Stir in the garlic and set aside.

When the potatoes are cooked, mash them until smooth and combine with the kale.

1 lb 2 oz (500 g) skinless salmon fillets
1 lb 10 oz (750 g) potatoes
8 large stalks of kale
1-2 tablespoons extra virgin olive oil
4 shallots/spring onions/ scallions, finely sliced
2 garlic cloves, finely chopped
Zest of 1 lemon
2 tablespoons finely chopped dill
1 tablespoon capers (optional)
Salt and freshly cracked black pepper
Lemon juice, for serving

Salmon Fishcakes with Sweet Chilli Yogurt (cont'd)

SWEET CHILLI YOGURT
1 cup (8 fl oz/250 ml)
    Greek unsweetened
    (strained plain) yogurt
1 tablespoon lemon juice
Sweet chilli sauce

Flake the salmon into small pieces and add to the kale and potatoes along with the lemon zest, dill and capers, if using. Season with salt and pepper to taste, and mix really well.

Divide the mixture into 8 equal rounds and pat into fishcakes. Place on the second prepared baking sheet and bake for 20-25 minutes, until golden.

Alternatively, shallow fry the fishcakes in a little extra virgin olive oil until golden on both sides.

To make the sweet chilli yogurt, mix the yogurt with the lemon juice then swirl in as much sweet chilli sauce as you like.

Serve the fishcakes with lemon juice and a dollop of the sweet chilli yogurt.

Tuna and Kale Mornay

I have been making tuna mornay for my family for years. It is only recently that I started adding the kale to it and now I would not even think of making it without it.

Thoroughly wash the kale. Remove and discard the thick lower part of the stalk and finely chop the leaves.

Preheat the oven to 180°C/350°F/Gas mark 4.

Drain the tuna, flake and place in a medium casserole.

Melt the butter in a small pan then stir in the flour and curry powder to form a roux.

Slowly pour in the milk, stirring constantly until the sauce starts to thicken and bubble. Season with salt and pepper, then stir in the cheese and cook for 1–2 minutes, until the cheese has melted into the sauce and the sauce is smooth, thick and bubbly.

Stir in the kale and keep stirring until the kale has wilted, cook for another 2–3 minutes.

Pour the sauce over the tuna and mix thoroughly to combine.

In a separate bowl, lightly crush the cornflakes and mix with the extra cheese. Cover the top of the tuna with the cornflake mixture.

Bake for 15–20 minutes, until golden and bubbly.

6-8 stalks cavolo nero (Tuscan kale)

14½ oz (425g) can tuna in brine or spring water

1 oz (30 g) butter

3 tablespoons flour

1 teaspoon curry powder

2 cups (16 fl oz/500 ml) milk

Salt and pepper

½ cup (4 oz/115 g) Cheddar (tasty) cheese, grated, plus an extra ¾ cup (6 oz/175 g) extra for the topping

3 cups (2 oz/60 g) cornflakes

Note: For a gluten/wheat free alternative use quinoa flour instead of regular wheaten flour. It works just as well in this recipe. The other ingredients in the recipe need to be checked for any gluten/wheat additives.

Index

Index